Criterion

The celebrated film director François Truffaut once famously observed that there was a certain incompatibility between the terms British and cinema. That was typical of the critical disparagement for so long suffered by British films. As late as 1969 a respected film scholar could dub British cinema 'the unknown cinema'. This was the situation because up to that time the critics, scholars and intellectuals writing about cinema preferred either continental films or latterly Hollywood to the homegrown product. Over the past thirty years that position has changed dramatically. There are now books, journals, courses and conferences entirely devoted to British cinema and a wider audience for British films, now accessible on screen, on video and DVD.

The Tauris British Film Guide series seeks to add to that process of revaluation by assessing in depth key British films from the past hundred years. The series will draw on all genres and all eras and will over time build into a wide-ranging library of informed, in-depth, readable books on the films that have defined British cinema. It is a publishing project that will comprehensively refute Truffaut's ill-informed judgement and demonstrate the variety, creativity, humanity, poetry and mythic power of the best of British cinema.

JEFFREY RICHARDS
General Editor, the British Film Guides

British Film Guides published and forthcoming:

THE BRITISH FILM GUIDE 5

The Charge of the Light Brigade

MARK CONNELLY

I.B. TAURIS

LONDON · NEW YORK

Published in 2003 by I.B. Tauris & Co. Ltd
6 Salem Road, London W2 4BU
175 Fifth Avenue, New York NY 10010
www.ibtauris.com

In the United States of America and Canada distributed by Palgrave
Macmillan, a division of St Martin's Press, 175 Fifth Avenue, New York
NY 10010

ISBN 1 86064 612 3

A full CIP record for this book is available from the British Library
A full CIP record for this book is available from the Library of Congress

Library of Congress catalog card: available

Set in Monotype Fournier and Univers Black by Ewan Smith, London
Printed and bound in Great Britain by MPG Books, Bodmin

Contents

Illustrations

Numbers 1, 3 and 4, behind-the-scenes production shots, are reproduced by courtesy of the British Film Institute. Numbers 2, 5 and 6 are reproduced by courtesy of the Ronald Grant Archive.

Acknowledgements

My first thanks go to Jeffrey Richards for inviting me to take part in this series and for all his help and constructive advice. Secondly, I would like to thank Kevin Brownlow, Vanessa Redgrave, David Watkin and Charles Wood for giving up their time in order to help me. An excellent day was spent at David Watkin's house; he provided lunch and a stream of memories and facts. We watched Kevin Brownlow's fascinating home movie of the production. It was curiously moving to see Tony Richardson holding the hands of his daughters, Joely and Natasha, David Hemmings larking about with the boom mike and Trevor Howard having his moustache trimmed! I would also like to thank Mark Glancy and the members of the Issues in Film History seminar at the Institute of Historical Research for giving me the chance to present a paper on my research. The responses and queries on the piece were very helpful. Lastly, I would like to thank my parents for being such film nuts in the first place and introducing me to so many different types of film. I remember seeing *The Charge of the Light Brigade* as a boy. It was on television one Christmas, about 1978 I think. It was one of those films my parents would sit down to watch, want me and my brother to watch with them, and would then intersperse it with their own memories of seeing it on its original release. What an introduction! Thanks.

Historical Note

Although the history of the Crimean campaign will necessarily be referred to throughout the following text, a brief outline of the basic facts may be useful.

The immediate cause of the war was the refusal of the Turks to accept Russian demands to protect Christians within the Ottoman Empire. At the same time the French were supporting the rights of the Catholic Church over access to the Holy Places in Palestine, which created tension with the Russian championing of the Orthodox monks in the region. On the wider stage Britain was fearful of Russian expansion in Eastern Europe and any possible push towards the eastern Mediterranean.

The Turks declared war on 23 September 1853 and began a campaign in the Danubian Provinces. On 30 November the Russians destroyed the Turkish fleet at Sinope. This caused the British and French to send warships to the area to fend off a possible Russian invasion. War between Russia and the British and French followed in March 1854. In September, the allies landed in the Crimea and besieged Sebastopol for a year. Before Sebastopol could be invested, the allies fought in a series of battles: Alma, Balaclava and Inkerman. The Charge of the Light Brigade was part of the Battle of Balaclava. Of the 673 cavalry men sent to attack the Russian positions, 247 were killed or wounded and over 500 horses died. The action was the result of a poorly-worded order from the British commander, Lord Raglan, and the vicious, and long-standing, quarrel between the British cavalry commander, Lord Lucan, and his subordinate in charge of the Light Brigade, Lord Cardigan. These threads combined to send the men charging down the wrong valley against the wrong objectives, thus incurring disastrous losses. The war then settled into a long siege of the Russia naval base at Sebastopol. As it dragged on, appalling administrative blunders were exposed in the British army. The treatment of the sick became a particularly notorious example and led to the dispatch of Florence Nightingale and her nurses to Turkey.

In January 1855, Cavour, the Prime Minister of Piedmont, sent 10,000 men to assist the allies in order to enhance his nation's international prestige. A truce followed when the Austrians threatened to join the war against Russia. A final peace was established at the Congress of Paris in March 1856.

The Crimean War was a major upheaval in mid-Victorian Britain. It was, at first, supported vigorously by the British public and men flocked to the colours. The industrial revolution ensured that the war not only reflected developments in weapons, but was also reported as never before. Photography allowed the British public to see the actual battle-field and the electric telegraph allowed press men to wire home their reports, giving a much greater immediacy to information. Thanks to men like William Howard Russell of *The Times*, people at home could read about the battles within a day of the action. What they read created mixed feelings. British troops fought with great skill and bravery at the battles of the Alma and Inkerman. But these achievements were mixed with incredible blunders, the most famous of which was, of course, the Charge of the Light Brigade at Balaclava. The British army proved to be inefficiently led, inefficiently supplied and incompetent to a startling degree. When the freezing Crimean winter descended in 1854, the British forces were reduced to a shambling wreck thanks to a lack of supplies and transport. The scandal shocked Britain and led to the resignation of the Prime Minister, Lord Aberdeen. British prestige was dented and there was a sense of introspection.

To many it appeared to highlight the irony that Britain, the mightiest industrial giant in the world, was so inefficiently governed that it could not organise its armies correctly. The war also came at a moment when the condition of the working class and the way in which Britain was governed were being debated. It was a period of tension as the British class system was solidifying in the maturing industrial and urbanised society. For the British middle class, the call of reform was a rallying cry; reform of the old gang of aristocrats who were holding up British progress. From the working classes the call was for better working conditions and representation in Parliament. The Crimean War therefore provides a lesson about nineteenth-century Britain in concentrated detail.

FURTHER READING

Geoffrey Best, *Mid-Victorian Britain*, London, 1979.
Denis Judd, *The Crimean War*, London, 1976.
A. W. Kinglake, *The Invasion of the Crimea* (8 vols), London, 1863–87.
William Howard Russell, *The British Expedition to the Crimea*, London, 1858.
Cecil Woodham-Smith, *The Reason Why*, London, 1953.

Film Credits

THE CHARGE OF THE LIGHT BRIGADE

Production Company	United Artists/Woodfall
Producer	Neil Hartley
Director	Tony Richardson
Screenplay	Charles Wood
Photography	David Watkin (Panavision/DeLuxe Color)
Camera Operator	Alan McCabe
Sound	Simon Kaye
Colour and Period Consultant	Lila de Nobili
Music	John Addison
Editors	Kevin Brownlow and Hugh Raggerts
Art Director	Edward Marshall
Costumes	David Walker
Special Effects	Robert MacDonald and Paul Pollard
Animation	Richard Williams
Historical Research	John Mollo
Production Supervisor	Roy Stevens
Production Manager	Julian Mackintosh
2nd Unit Director	Christian de Chalonge
Assistant Director	Clive Reed
2nd Unit Photographer	Peter Suschitzky
Continuity	Angela Allen
Length	12,690 ft
Running Time	132 minutes
UK Première	10 April 1968
US Première	14 April 1968

CAST

Trevor Howard	Lord Cardigan
Vanessa Redgrave	Clarissa
John Gielgud	Lord Raglan
Harry Andrews	Lord Lucan
Jill Bennett	Mrs Duberly
David Hemmings	Captain Nolan

Ben Aris	Maxse
Micky Baker	Trooper Metcalfe
Peter Bowles	Paymaster Duberly
Leo Britt	General Scarlett
Mark Burns	Captain Morris
John Carney	Trooper Mitchell
Helen Cherry	Lady Scarlett
Christopher Chittell	Trooper
Ambrose Coghill	Douglas
Chris Cunningham	Farrier
Mark Dignam	General Airey
Alan Dobie	Mogg
Georges Douking	Marshal St Arnaud
Andrew Faulds	Quaker Preacher
Derek Fuke	Trooper
Willoughby Goddard	Squire
John Hallam	Officer
Barbara Hicks	Mrs Duberly's Maid
Ben Howard	Pridmore
Rachel Kempson	Mrs Codrington
T. P. McKenna	William Howard Russell
Howard Marion-Crawford	Sir George Brown
Michael Miller	Major-General Sir Colin Campbell
Declan Mulholland	Farrier
Roger Mutton	Rupert Codrington
Valerie Newman	Mrs Mitchell
Roy Patterson	Regimental Sergeant Major
Corin Redgrave	Featherstonehaugh
Norman Rossington	Sergeant Major Corbett
Dino Shafeek	Indian Servant
John Treneman	Sergeant Smith
Colin Vancao	Captain Chateris
Donald Wolfit	Macbeth
Peter Woodthorpe	Valet

Available on Connoisseur Video (Widescreen). Catalogue Number: CR094.

Introduction

The Charge of the Light Brigade was the most expensive British film ever made when it came out in 1968. Its director, Tony Richardson, was one of the most important innovators in British theatre and had a list of highly praised and significant films to his credit. His wife at the time was the committed left-wing activist Vanessa Redgrave, who was to play a role in the film. Alongside her was one of the glamour boys of the 1960s, David Hemmings. These young stars were complemented by some of the finest, established acting talents, John Gielgud and Trevor Howard. Generational gaps were bridged in the casting of the film.

Britain in 1968 was a society witnessing social, cultural and economic changes. In this milieu a film based on a famous historical incident was released. At first glance this seems almost surreal. Why make a large-scale costume drama at such a moment; what relevance and appeal could it have? As Charles Wood's wonderful script was to show, the world of 1854 actually had some strong parallels with that of Britain in the 1960s.

The Charge of the Light Brigade was also made at a time when Hollywood was making large investments in British ventures. Films great and small were being made in Britain by British talent but with Hollywood money. *The Charge of the Light Brigade* represented the apogee of this commitment – and also marked the beginning of the end.

By the time it was released the film was already well known, verging on the notorious. Because Richardson had courted controversy, the film has never received the attention it deserved. Few directors have been subject to so much critical vitriol as Tony Richardson. Some of the criticism has been helpful, providing insights into a rather enigmatic figure, but much of it has actually clouded the issue and has allowed a flabby orthodoxy to grow up surrounding his work. The basic accusation is that his work was confused, inconsistent and ill-constructed. It is the intention of this book to question whether this is, in fact, the case. Perfection may not have been within Richardson's grasp, but just how much of a handicap was this? This work will seek to explore the film, highlighting its strengths and weaknesses.

The book is divided into three main sections. Chapter 1 looks at the context, examining Richardson's earlier career and the 'road to *The Charge*'. It also looks at British society in the 1960s and seeks to show the world that produced *The Charge*. In the second chapter the narrative and nature of the film itself will be examined. The final chapter looks at the critical reception of the film at the time and its reputation since.

It will already be clear that what follows is the reaction of a fan of the film. However, it is not intended to be an uncritical examination. *The Charge of the Light Brigade* deserves a reassessment. Let's sound the charge!

ONE
The Context

Few people would doubt that over the last few years the 1960s and 1970s have achieved a new cult status in Britain, particularly among the nation's youth. Pop groups reel off cover versions of the hits of the time, imitate the fashions of the period and hint that they are as sexually promiscuous and demanding as earlier icons. The recent Spice Girls movie, *Spice World*, was obviously a pastiche of the Beatles' movies *A Hard Day's Night* and *Help!*. Advertising is for ever making sly references to the great and popular movies of the period. In recent years products have been advertised using either clips lifted directly from, or reconstructions of, *The Italian Job*, *Bullitt* and *Easy Rider*. Michael Caine is certainly a rediscovered hero, symbolising for many young people a cocky, assured and quick-fire persona. Everyone knows, and can repeat like a mantra, his two now famous lines from *The Italian Job*: 'You were only supposed to blow the bloody doors off' and 'It's all right lads, I've got a plan'. The flamboyant dectectives, crime-fighting heroes and protectors of western society of the age have also had a renaissance. *Jason King*, *The Saint*, *The Avengers*, *Mission Impossible* have come back as *Austin Powers* and in movies based directly on the original programmes. A cult of kitsch, extravagance and seemingly effortless style and sex appeal is firmly back with us. For most young people today, Michael Caine in a white shirt overlaid with florid purple flowers with rounded, soft, massive collars topped by a flowing leather jacket is the 1960s. It is a far cry from the Michael Caine of *The Ipcress File* – Harry Palmer in hard-edged black spectacles, a tight, dark suit, with a narrow tie, polished shoes and a Burberry mac. In short, the popular memory of the 1960s is one that actually begins around 1968.

In 1968 Tony Richardson's much-talked about *The Charge of the Light Brigade* was released. Although it is an historical film, set in the 1850s, the look of the movie is exactly that of the popular memory of the late 1960s. Just how far is it from the cover of *Sgt Pepper's Lonely*

Hearts Club Band? For the gorgeous, gaudy uniforms, floppy haircuts and flamboyant moustaches and side-whiskers suggest that it could be set not just in the Crimea in 1854 but equally well in a boutique on the King's Road.

Cecil Antonio Richardson was born on 5 June 1928 in Saltaire, York-shire.[1] He was raised by a raft of female relations and received lavish attention from his maternal grandmother and one of his aunts. After a schooling befitting a lower-middle-class Yorkshire boy – a minor public school with an inflated idea of its own worth – he went up to Oxford where he continued to express his passion for the theatre. Richardson realised early on that his real interest and talent lay in directing. Such was his enthusiasm for the stage that he was theatre critic for the university journal, *Isis*, and the first student to be president of both the Oxford University Experimental Theatre Club and the Oxford University Dramatic Society.

In 1951 he went down from Oxford straight to London intent on a career within the performing arts. After scraping a living in various jobs on the fringes of the theatrical world, Richardson founded the English Stage Company at the Royal Court Theatre, Sloane Square, with a group of like-minded friends.

The company was catapulted to glory and given an enduring, legendary reputation by John Osborne's play *Look Back in Anger*, produced at the Court in 1956. Richardson directed Kenneth Haigh, Mary Ure, Alan Bates and Helena Hughes in the original production which opened on 8 May. *Look Back in Anger* has since achieved an iconic, and undoubtedly somewhat clichéd, status. It is regarded as the moment when a standard of rebellion was planted firmly on the brow of English life and especially on the moribund English stage. Osborne and Richardson are said to have brought to life the resentments of 'angry young men'. Angry at finding Britain a petrifying, stultifying society. Angry at a Britain that did not seem to represent anything, or if it did finding those values worthless and mean. Angry at not having a cause to die for. It is therefore well worth remembering that the play was by no means immediately universally acclaimed. Only once the heavyweight critics of the heavy-weight Sunday newspapers, Harold Hobson of the *Sunday Times* and Ken Tynan of the *Observer*, had expressed their approval did the atmosphere change. Richardson wrote in his autobiography: 'They made us the theatre of the moment, the place where it was happening – take it or leave it, love it or hate it.'[2]

A year later the company scored a great success with John Osborne's *The Entertainer*. Laurence Olivier played the role of the seedy music-hall comedian slipping into oblivion along with the halls themselves. It was a metaphor for a nation that had just witnessed the Suez fiasco, and had been forced to realise it too was living on past glories that could no longer be sustained in the modern world. The metaphorical message of the play, bound up in the wider debate over Suez and whether Britain had the right to dictate policy to other nations, was later to be an important theme of *The Charge of the Light Brigade*.

Having a long-standing interest in the idea of filming *Look Back in Anger*, Richardson got the chance in 1958. It was not his first taste of film direction, for in 1955 he had made *Momma Don't Allow* with Karel Reisz, a short documentary about life in and around North London jazz clubs. Lindsay Anderson, a passionate believer in new approaches to cinema and a fresh understanding of the nature of documentary films, brought together a clutch of similar films and launched Free Cinema. The Free Cinema group showed their films as a series at the National Film Theatre in February 1956. Shown alongside *Momma Don't Allow* were Anderson's *O Dreamland* and Lorenza Mazzetti's *Together*. The film-makers signed a manifesto, drafted by Anderson:

> As film-makers we believe that
> > No film can be too personal
> > The image speaks. Sound amplifies and comments. Size is irrelevant.
> Perfection is not the aim.[3]

Elements of this manifesto were to infuse all of Richardson's films.

Anderson was establishing a clique of angry young film-makers at just the moment when Osborne was establishing the angry young men of the theatre. Tony Richardson was the man with a foot in both camps.

The chance to make a film version of *Look Back in Anger* came when the Canadian producer Harry Saltzman decided to take a chance on the project. From the agreement came a production company, Woodfall. (It was named after the Chelsea street in which John and Mary Ure lived.) Saltzman managed to persuade Warner Brothers to finance the project, largely because Richard Burton had expressed an interest in the lead role of Jimmy Porter.

The film received mixed reviews when it was released. Leonard Mosley, critic of the *Daily Express*, posed a question: 'How long does it take a sensational, shocking and timely play to become easily digestible and mildly dated? Answer: the time it takes to transfer it from the stage to the screen.'[4] Though a valid point, it was also a somewhat snobbish one. The vast majority of British cinema-goers were not regular attenders of the theatre and though they probably knew of the ragings of Jimmy Porter had had no chance to witness them. *Look Back in Anger* did not mark an entirely new direction for British cinema, but it certainly gave the cinema-going public a chance to witness the growing phenomenon of the 'kitchen sink' drama for themselves.

Richardson followed *Look Back in Anger* with a filmed version of *The Entertainer* (1960). It was a curious subject for a film, with Olivier re-creating his stage role of Archie Rice and the peeling wallpaper of the seaside theatres and thinning crowds entering them all duly reproduced. But the film has no great appeal. The staginess of *Look Back in Anger* was overcome by Burton's bravura performance and youthful, sexually potent appeal. Though Olivier played his role with great skill, it was a character hardly likely to strike a chord with young cinema audiences. Woodfall was plunged into a perilous financial state by the even more modest box-office success of *The Entertainer*.

At this point Richardson shelved some projects and accepted an invitation from 20th Century-Fox to direct an adaptation of William Faulkner's *Sanctuary* in Hollywood. However, Woodfall was not left to stew; Karel Reisz was approached to direct a screen version of Alan Sillitoe's novel *Saturday Night and Sunday Morning*. Even more than *Look Back in Anger*, *Saturday Night and Sunday Morning* set the cinema benchmark for kitchen sink dramas. Albert Finney attacked with relish his role as Arthur Seaton. Reisz captured the boredom, aggression and energy wrapped up in Seaton. He balanced him against the industrial landscape of Nottingham, ironically placed within sight of rolling hills and fields. A truly cinematic vision was much easier to create from a novel than from the theatrical conventions of either *Look Back in Anger* or *The Entertainer*. With very little spent on publicity, Woodfall was delighted to find it had scored a hit. The film took more than £100,000 and paved the way for a more ambitious follow-up.[5]

Richardson wanted to make an all-location film and he now had the money to do it. The desire to work outdoors and in the genuine locations was an obsession Richardson never lost, and was a key element of *The Charge of the Light Brigade*. His version of Shelagh Delaney's *A Taste of Honey* (1961) took elements of the realism of *Saturday Night and Sunday Morning*, but was not really of the same cloth. It does not have the harshness of Reisz's film. A feeling of fantasy pervades the film and the title is not as ironic as it might at first seem. Robert Murphy believes that *A Taste of Honey* achieves the 'poetic realism' of Free Cinema more fully than any other film made by Reisz or Anderson.[6] *A Taste of Honey* was also a commercial success and gave Richardson even more confidence to experiment.

Woodfall's next project was an adaptation of Sillitoe's short story, *The Loneliness of the Long Distance Runner* (1962). Tom Courtenay gave an excellent performance as Colin, the young criminal rebelling against the codes and conventions of his society. Colin's rebellion was even more effective than Seaton's, for whereas Finney's bulk always gave the impression of a man who could get his way by sheer physical force, Courtenay's wiry frame meant that the rebellion had to be mental as well as physical. As a result it is both more effective and rather chilling.

Richardson was always assured in his stage direction. In his theatrical career he had gained a repuation as a careful and thoughtful director. The look and lighting of the set were extremely important to his idea of the overall feel. He brought this approach to his films and applied the techniques and skills of the French *nouvelle vague*. The *nouvelle vague* film-makers laid great stress on the importance of personal attachment to a project and independence from 'traditional' studio styles and practices. *Auteur*, the imprint of the director, was therefore very much at the heart of the movement. It also often meant a fresh understanding of cimematic conventions on sex, sexuality and social relationships. This was clearly seen in *The Loneliness of the Long Distance Runner*. Probably because it was such a bold experiment, Richardson was roundly condemned by the press. In particular the trade and specialist press was whipped up to something close to fury. For *Sight and Sound* it was a triumph of style over substance and it was a style it hated.[7] By its use of camera techniques, editing, lighting and overall style, *The Loneliness of the Long Distance Runner* has far more of the feel of a 1960s film. By that I mean it is probably the first movie of the decade to show some of the elements the popular memory associates with it: cocky working-class characters with distinct accents, an obvious interest in sex, and rebellion against the traditional codes of 'conformist' society.

But no matter how different *Saturday Night and Sunday Morning* is to *The Loneliness of the Long Distance Runner* in terms of texture and look, the films are often taken together. Indeed, they are gathered with such films as *A Kind of Loving* (1962), *Billy Liar* (1963) and *This Sporting Life* (1963). Though it can be pointed out that they are in fact very different types of film and have only their northern settings linking them, this runs the risk of ignoring why they were originally grouped together. Novelty linked these films, the novelty of seeing working-class people on their own terms, in their own worlds, applying their own ways of living. It was a new departure in its intensity.

Where do such films stand in the popular understanding of the 1960s? Put simply they don't. We can see the '60s as having two halves. One explored the lives of the long neglected northern working class. The other celebrated the values of 'Swinging' London. In the popular imagination only one-half has real life: the second. Robert Murphy has questioned such simplistic understandings. He argues that the Swinging London films of the second half of the decade often have darker, introspective and more questioning sides to them too which have been ignored.[8] Fascinatingly, Richardson was involved in every twist and turn of this debate. He directed the first kitchen sink play, *Look Back in Anger*, produced the first great kitchen sink film, *Saturday Night and Sunday Morning*, and then directed the first film to establish many of the cinematic conventions of later 1960s British cinema, *The Loneliness of the Long Distance Runner*.

Richardson was also one of the instigators of the fashion for wearing pastiche historical costume, for in 1963 his adaptation of *Tom Jones* was released. John Osborne adapted and condensed Henry Fielding's 1749 novel. Finney took the leading role and Richardson directed it with tremendous gusto, gimmickry and style which brought out the best of Walter Lassally's skill as a cameraman. Planned as a lavish, full-colour romp, it was always going to be an expensive production and brought United Artists into partnership with Woodfall. The same partnership later made *The Charge of the Light Brigade*.

Sex is at the heart of *Tom Jones*; it is saucy, bawdy and erotic. The film also celebrates women who are interested in sex, a variation on the usual approach in which sexual desire was acceptable in men but somehow dangerous in women. Blushing virgins are not thick on the ground in *Tom Jones*. Finney's performance was far removed from that of *Saturday Night and Sunday Morning*. Though both Arthur Seaton and Tom Jones are energetic young men, Jones has no angst, existentialist or otherwise, he is an earthy, rumbustious figure. *Tom Jones* was a pantomime for the 1960s and it set a new agenda for the decade. But in British cinema costume drama had always been a good cover for sex, as can be seen in films such as *The Private Life of Henry VIII*, *Nell Gwyn* and *The Wicked Lady*. It was in comparison to the increasingly stale costume dramas of the 1950s that *Tom Jones* was a new departure. *Ivanhoe*, *Kidnapped* and

Quentin Durward may have had love and romance interests, but there was hardly a sex interest.[9] The closest comparator with *Tom Jones* was *The Beggar's Opera* (1952), but even here the sheer braggadocio of Gay's Macheath was downplayed. Escapism, colour, sex, comedy and cockiness were at the heart of *Tom Jones*. It suited an increasingly affluent society perfectly. More particularly, it suited the young, ordinary, increasingly affluent members of society perfectly. *Tom Jones* was a smash in the USA and did very good business in Britain too. Tony Richardson had become a golden boy. He was master of the northern industrial landscape and fantasies of London tavern life of the eighteenth century. For him cinema was not just the chance to question society, it was the chance to write something big, to paint huge canvases using the cleverest of techniques. It was a chance to delight the ear with sharp dialogue, captivate the eye by revealing grand, strange, detailed and glorious visions. It was a chance to say something personal to a large audience. It was screen poetry, occasionally bawdy, occasionally indistinct, but fresh and committed.

To what extent was the 1960s a decade of sexual freedom and promiscuity? If we refer to our popular stereotype again, the '60s is seen as a time of orgies, love-ins, the pill, of free, uncomplicated sex. Further, it is thought that the cinema proved, validated, encouraged and reflected this. Parliamentary Acts certainly appear to confirm that changes were occuring in attitudes towards sex, with a rush coming in 1967 – the Abortion Act, the National Health Service (family planning) Act and the Sexual Offences Act (legalising homosexual acts between two consenting adults in private). This sudden clustering of legislation was not the result of an equally sudden conversion, but of many years of slow but sure change. *Tom Jones* was one of the indicators of the change and *The Charge of the Light Brigade* also reflected changing and emerging attitudes towards sex. But did cinema give free affirmation to free love? Films such as *Alfie* (1966), *Here We Go Round the Mulberry Bush* (1967), *Up the Junction* (1967) and *Blow-Up* (1966) seem to confirm that they did. Once again Robert Murphy argues otherwise, he sees disturbing undertones in many of the films that are often taken as simply hedonistic tributes to Swinging London.[10] What cannot be doubted, however, is the association of Terence Stamp, Michael Caine and David Hemmings with suave, good-looking playboys, wideboys and generally cheeky chappies who have a way with the girls.

This association has become a part of our popular culture and has coloured our view of the '60s and its cinema. From this viewpoint the comedian Harry Enfield wickedly satirised the period in his television show. We see the film *Poppet on a Swing*, which established the 'reputation of young Michael Hemmingstamp as one of Swinging London's most lovable shits'. The 'film' opens with a girl on a swing in a park. Enfield wanders over to her. His most noticeable feature is a huge mop of blond hair. Grabbing the chains of the swing he starts laughing wildly, crying, 'Faster, faster, you bitch', while the camera rapidly cuts from a close-up of his face to a close-up of her. He then tells her he will take her to a party. Standing by an open-topped sports car, he remarks that it's a present 'from the shit. My father, he's the shit.' At the party his friend says that she has 'nice boobs'. The scene cuts to a post-coital cigarette. Enfield asks her whether it was her first time, she says yes and he replies, 'Thought so, you weren't very good were you?' Pushing her out of bed, he tells her to do the washing up on her way out. We then find out that the girl is pregnant. Enfield drives her back to her family house, telling her father that his daughter is 'up the spout', and therefore 'no good to me'. Driving off he sees a girl walking down the street. Pulling over he calls, 'Get in, you bitch', and the credits roll. It is a perfect pastiche of our perfectly clichéd understanding and popular memory of 1960s cinema. David Hemmings, Michael Caine and Terence Stamp are identified as *the* actors of the period and sexual power, linked to misogyny, are seen to be their trademarks. *The Charge of the Light Brigade* can be used to test this assumption.

The extent to which the '60s were truly revolutionary years is open to debate, but it cannot be denied that things were changing and questions were being asked about traditional codes and standards. Traditional figures of authority and stability were certainly under increasing pressure. The satirical stabs of BBC television's *That was the Week that was* were far sharper than 1950s cinema satire. Films like *Lucky Jim* (1957) can hardly be called satire, the Boulting brothers transformed Kingsley Amis's piquant sketch of an English university into a knock-about farce. Another Boulting brothers piece, *Private's Progress* (1956), had few punches (especially when compared to their much sharper *I'm All Right Jack* [1959]), while Launder and Gilliat's so-called political satire *Left, Right and Centre* (1959) is plain feeble.

As the establishment, its methods, codes and personnel came under more scrutiny and questioning, it seems natural that the ever-declining British Empire and the British army should come in for a degree of examination. Sixties films about Britain's history, its armed forces and the empire are, however, an eclectic and odd bunch. Army and empire

were very firmly linked in Cy Endfield's *Zulu* (1964), the film that gave
Michael Caine his big break. Ironically, given Caine's later stereotyped
image, he played an upper-class officer in this film, born to lead men.
The nature of the army and the forced expansion of the British Empire
is, of course, highlighted in this film, but it is far from being a bitter
critique. The army was presented as a harsh, disciplined environment,
but it is this core of professional discipline that saves it from the attacks
of the Zulus. Urban working class misfits and rural Welsh farmers
combine in the ranks of privates under brave and resourceful officers.
The combination saves them from an overwhelming Zulu onslaught. At
the end of the film the incredibly brave young Zulu warriors have learned
to respect their foes and vice versa. The Zulus retreat chanting praise to
their worthy adversaries. *Zulu* is a macho film, it celebrates male values,
but it cannot be labelled a bigoted or satirical movie. The British Empire
is not really questioned and codes of honour, chivalry even, are respected.
Not what one would expect from a 'typical' '60s movie.

Closer to the popular myth are films like Richard Lester's *How I Won
the War* (1967). The attitudes of officers and men were wickedly sent up,
and other ranks are cringingly inferior to their brave, paternalistic
officers. A sketch from the popular radio show of the time, *I'm Sorry I'll
Read That Again*, parodied the prisoner of war movie genre. The German
camp commandant, played by John Cleese, calls forward the usual bunch
of 'lovable cockney privates'. They introduce themselves as 'Titch',
'Nobby', 'Ginger' and 'Chalky'. The spirit was exactly that of Lester's
film. Even that most traditionally British of genres, the Carry Ons,
joined the jokes against army and empire. *Carry On Up the Khyber* (1968)
revealed the British army to be a bungling bunch of clowns, while the
diplomats and colonial rulers are crooks and bounders. Sid James played
his usual role as a spiv, only this time he was Sir Sydney Ruff-Diamond,
governor of a north-west frontier province. But it should be noted that
the humour is affectionate, end-of-the-pier stuff; it is not biting satire.
British *sang froid* is parodied gloriously when a dinner party goes on as
if nothing is happening, despite the fact that rebellious tribesmen are
shelling the residency. When Sir Sydney's aide-de-camp asks him what
they should do about the situation he replies, 'Do? Do? We're British,
we'll do nothing until it's too late.'

New ideas about war and empire were partly the result of the increasingly problematic question of American intervention in Vietnam. In
common with sections of American society, British students, artists,
political activists and academics became involved in debate over the

1. *Turkish soldiers played the thin red line. They are seen here relaxing between scenes.*

wisdom and morality of western interference in Vietnam. The questioning of America's role was reflected in the cinema. In 1970, for example, two impressive Westerns, *Soldier Blue* and *Little Big Man*, depicted scenes of massacres of aboriginal Americans. Both appear to invert the conventions of the usual 7th Cavalry/Western genre to make critical, allegorical statements about Vietnam.

As well as adopting a more satirical approach, war films departed from the unquestioning heroics and honourable codes that had been their earlier trademark. *The Hill* (1965) showed the brutality of an army prison in which men are treated like rubbish and are locked away for the most insignificant reasons. *Play Dirty* (1968) starred Michael Caine as a Second World War 'hero' who succeeds because he abandons all the usual codes to play dirty. *The Charge of the Light Brigade* included many similar elements and it can be argued that Richardson's film represented the peak of this radical revisionism.

However, it is certainly not the case that patriotism had become a dirty word and that association with Britishness was something to be avoided at all costs. There was a flip-side to the coin. First, as in our own times, the nation was obsessed with the Second World War and British cinema continued to churn out 'standard' World War Two movies, many of which did good box-office business: *Where Eagles Dare* (1969), *Mosquito Squadron* (1968), *Attack on the Iron Coast* (1967), *633 Squadron* (1964) and the huge, rambling, but ultimately impressive *The Battle of Britain* (1969). Secondly, patriotism and modernity merged to create the original Cool Britannia, the feel-good sense of self-confident brashness so desired by pop groups and New Labour to this day. In 1966 England won the World Cup and they won it in red shirts. As Alf Garnett said, it was a trick to make you think Harold 'Bloody' Wilson had won the World Cup for you. Football, sexiness and a left-wing patriotism came together in a way Tony Blair must dream about. Swinging London seemed to set the tone for Swinging Britain. Carnaby Street, the King's Road and Mary Quant became the last word in fashion, wresting control from Milan and Paris. Twiggy symbolised the new dominance of Britain on the world's catwalk.

All of these elements came together in the swansong of the decade, *The Italian Job*. British style invaded the continent in every sense. British gangsters outwit the mafia; British cars out manoeuvre the Fiats of the Italian police; England and its supporters arrive in Turin for the football international (the use of Union flags to symbolise the English supporters reveals how British symbols could be hijacked by the English alone and are taken to be definitions of Englishness); English crooks look more stylish than the Italians and have a better way with the birds. (Women were always 'birds' in the 1960s.) Noël Coward resides in his cell, a guest of Her Majesty, but her most devoted servant too. He robs in the name of the country. When news gets back to England that Caine and the boys have got away with the loot, Coward walks down the galleries of the prison waving like Her Majesty. The other prisoners bash their cutlery on the rails saluting him and chant 'England'. The established queens meet the new ones and agree to be proud to be British/English. It is a theme continued to this day by the polished, slightly camp, self-consciously self-referential James Bond movies. Just where are the Grosvenor Square demonstrations against American intervention in Vietnam in all this?

The 1960s are therefore not easily quantifiable. At times reality approaches the stereotype and popular image – very few popular images are entirely bogus or based upon absolutely nothing. But it was a complex decade, questioning and liberating; seemingly radical and revolutionary at times but highly conservative and traditional at others. It was in this strange milieu that *The Charge of the Light Brigade* was created and shaped. Richardson was a man of his time and his film would show that. But he was also his own man with his own understanding of the power of cinema and his film would show that too.

Richardson's *The Charge of the Light Brigade* must be seen in context. By virtue of its sheer scale and cost it was an exceptional movie, and it set a standard for further Hollywood–British projects. As a costume drama it sat with a clutch of other movies, and the last two years of the decade saw a rush of films in this genre. As noted earlier, *Tom Jones* had revitalised the costume and historical drama. Historical dramas were regarded as good business, though they were often expensive and, in reality, did not recoup their outlay. Hollywood encouraged historical dramas, for its investment in the British industry was double-edged. It was only partly inspired by London's reputation as a city with a potent sense of fashion and style. The other part was the continued love affair with the grand yarns of British history. As a result the second half of the 1960s saw a boom in history films.

The sixteenth and seventeenth centuries were well represented, starting with the high-quality adaptation of Robert Bolt's play *A Man for All Seasons* (1966). Paul Scofield played Sir Thomas More and led an excellent cast, including Wendy Hiller as his wife and Robert Shaw who gave a bravura performance as the young Henry VIII. It is an interesting film in-so-far as it avoids simple vilification of Henry, but shows him to be a passionate young man. Susannah York and Corin Redgrave play More's daughter and prospective son-in-law. They are equally passionate in their opposition to Henry. The film therefore stresses the eagerness of youth to make its mark on the world. Their passions may be misplaced – just as those of some of the young characters in *The Charge of the Light Brigade* are – but at least they are committed and determined to change the world.

Passions of a more carnal nature were at the heart of *Anne of a Thousand Days* (1970). In this film about the brief ascendancy of Anne Boleyn, a much more traditional approach was taken. Henry is portrayed as a man driven by his sexual desire who, when he finds that he does not quite get his own way, develops an irrational hatred for his wife. In the same year, the grand historical epic *Cromwell* was released. Ken Hughes's screenplay occasionally takes extreme liberties with the historical record, but the look of the film is authentic. Richard Harris played Cromwell as a man of deep personal commitment and Alec Guinness played

Charles I as a man of deep personal insecurity and inconstancy. Cromwell's desire to purge and cleanse the old world has all the incandescence and enthusiasm of Captain Nolan in *The Charge of the Light Brigade*.

Closer to *The Charge of the Light Brigade* in terms of historical period was John Schlesinger's *Far from the Madding Crowd* (1967). A long, but undeniably beautiful film – Nic Roeg's photography of the Dorset countryside is ravishing – Schlesinger's adaptation of the Thomas Hardy novel cost a fortune ($4 million). It had further elements in common with *The Charge of the Light Brigade*, for it starred two young actors more in tune with Swinging London than the bucolic Dorset hills, Terence Stamp and Julie Christie. Robert Murphy has commented: 'It is difficult to shake off the feeling that at any moment they may discard their funny voices and fancy dress and rush off to a Chelsea party.'[11]

The decade closed with a remake of *Goodbye, Mr Chips*. It was a baffling decision. Just what sort of audience would there be for a film celebrating public school values when that same society had produced Lindsay Anderson's *If* …, a semi-fantastic and violent indictment of the system Mr Chips loved and symbolised? No fewer than four historical film/costume dramas were released in 1969. In complete contrast to the flabby sentimentality of *Goodbye, Mr Chips* (which lacks the charm and warmth of the original), was the strange *Alfred the Great*. David Hemmings played the king with great sensitivity. Clive Donner's script displayed how historical themes could have modern parallels, for the Anglo-Saxon world was marked by a debate about reason and conscience, about spirituality versus carnal and violent desires. British society at the end of the 1960s could relate to many of these concepts but, unfortunately, like *The Charge of the Light Brigade*, the film puzzled the critics and did not prove a box-office success.

The last few years of the decade also saw a wave of army/war films. Charles Wood wrote the screenplay for the Second World War drama, *The Long Day's Dying*. Like *The Charge of the Light Brigade*, it was released in 1968. The close links between the two films were confirmed by the appearances of David Hemmings and Alan Dobie in leading roles. Critics hated the film, finding in it much the same faults as they identified in *The Charge of the Light Brigade*. They were confused by the fact that it was an anti-war film which celebrated some of the values of war and army life. Wood was showing, as he did in *The Charge*, that war has a complex hold over the minds and imaginations of humans. That although it is ultimately an awful, destructive, wasteful process, it has inspired men and motivated them intellectually and emotionally. A simpler anti-war polemic was delivered by Richard Attenborough in *Oh! What a Lovely War* (1969). Attenborough portrayed the Great War as a farcical tragedy, expanding upon Joan Littlewood's original play in which the war was a ghastly pierrot show. He shot the whole film on Brighton pier, Brighton promenade and the South Downs. A massive, impressive, grotesque and very powerful movie, it was hampered by its extremely British temperament and appeal to the British memory of the war, thus making it almost impossible to capture the American market.

Richardson's satirical approach to the story of the Charge of the Light Brigade has much in common with the way in which the Great War was recast in the 1960s. The fiftieth anniversary commemorations of the Great War brought the conflict back to public attention. The BBC made a landmark documentary series, *The Great War*, and the war was examined in a sudden rush of books. Alan Clark set the new tone in 1961 with his work *The Donkeys*. The title encapsulated the atmosphere, for he indicted the British generals as donkeys who led heroes. Fascinatingly, he drew upon the Crimean War in his introduction: 'My generation did not fight in the Second World War. To many of us the First is as remote as the Crimean, its causes and its personnel obscure and disreputable.'[12] The Great War and the Crimea were linked as wars fought by disreputable men over disreputable causes in a past far, far away.

In complete opposition to this spirit of doubt and satire, as seen in Attenborough's bitter indictment of military folly, was *The Battle of Britain*, also released in 1969. Guy Hamilton's hugely expensive film for United Artists told the history of the aerial campaign over Britain with painstaking accuracy while confirming all the popular myths and legends of the period. As with *Oh! What a Lovely War* the entire panoply of British acting talent was assembled, including Laurence Olivier, Trevor Howard, Ralph Richardson, Robert Shaw, Michael Caine and Susannah York. The big budget screams at the viewer from the brilliant aerial scenes to the score by William Walton. Unfortunately, if *Oh! What a Lovely War* was too surreal and too shocking, *The Battle of Britain* seemed a bit too old-fashioned and a bit too ambitious for its own good. By the end of the decade, having spent fortunes on these films and not having recouped that much, the big Hollywood companies were questioning their commitment to Britain and were starting to pack up and head for home.

The costume/historical drama was at the heart of the big productions of the second half of the decade, but it has received precious little attention from serious film critics. Too many glib assumptions have been made about it, but by ignoring the historical dramas of the '60s, commentators have missed out on many interesting films. Like other costume dramas of the time, *The Charge of the Light Brigade* was committed, ambitious yet ambiguous. It was a film of its time and a parable for its time but it was also a film intent on capturing the spirit of a past age, a spirit that could not easily be quantified and labelled.

Richardson's choice of the Charge of the Light Brigade as a topic for a film may at first glance appear odd. It certainly appears to confirm the claims of those who argue that his career was nothing but an erratic lurching from pillar to post. The success of *Tom Jones* was not followed by work of equal critical or box-office acclaim. *The Loved One* (1965) was an uneven attempt to bring the deliciously sharp prose of Evelyn Waugh to cinematic life. Two 'arty' movies, *Mademoiselle* and *The Sailor from Gibraltar*, were bold in conception and once again revealed his ability to capture the style of French cinema, but were hardly likely to prove broadly popular. *The Red and the Blue* was a mad 30-minute musical, starring Michael York and Vanessa Redgrave (whom Richardson had married in 1962). Once again it is impossible not to admire his audacity, but these films could hardly be expected to bring the money rolling in. Given this commitment to the experimental, a project based on the Charge of the Light Brigade looks odd indeed. Kevin Brownlow, the editor of *The Charge of the Light Brigade*, certainly felt it was out of character. In April 1968 he scribbled some notes about his role in the production: 'I was flabbergasted when Tony Richardson began work on his version. He was totally the wrong director. He needs a small canvas, I felt, an intimate drama. He has no feeling for sweeping spectacle, a military life.'[13]

In his autobiography Richardson pointed out that he was a keen student of history, even though he had studied English at university. He was also passionately interested in strange and exotic locations, an interest he linked to a visit to see a stage version of *Around the World in Eighty Days* as a child. When combined with his interest in Shakespeare and his history plays, the attraction to the charge becomes less perplexing. The Charge of the Light Brigade took place in a strange location and has an air of grand, quixotic tragedy about it that Shakespeare would have found fascinating. It was certainly not a subject Richardson could have approached without a great deal of mental baggage, for the charge has a peculiar role in British history, reflecting a peculiar aspect of British national identity. It has become an expression of our culture.

The Charge of the Light Brigade took place on 25 October 1856 near Balaclava on the Crimean peninsula. The first knowledge the British public had of the event was via the pages of *The Times*. William Howard Russell, the first modern war correspondent, flashed home his report on the electric telegraph. Disaster was wrapped up in the story of the wider battle of Balaclava, but it was impossible not to notice that of the 700 men who had charged down the valley only 195 had returned and 500 horses had been killed. Once Roger Fenton's photographs had been sent home, it was possible for Victorians to see the place of disaster as well as read about it. The shock of this particular disaster was, however, only one in a catalogue for the British during the Crimean War that is now common knowledge largely thanks to the bitter commentary of Russell.

Though the charge was an undoubted disaster, it was soon being subtly recast as a story of heroism in spite of the odds, a story far more palatable to all concerned. Tennyson confirmed this reorientation with his poem *The Charge of the Light Brigade*, which became famous throughout the world.

Blundering and heroism slowly achieved the status of cultural touchstones for the British. The process appears to be a counterpart to Martin Wiener's idea of British cultural failure. He argues that success became embarrassing to the British, they grew ashamed of having a tradesman-like culture and so adopted the way of the aristocrat and the amateur instead, thus losing the economic lead achieved earlier in the nineteenth century.[14] A crucial cultural concept grew up, seemingly proving that the British have become wedded to an idea of gentlemanly codes and a lack of professionalism which leads to disasters. George Orwell's examination of the national character, 'The Lion and the Unicorn' (1940), commented on this trait. For him it proved a hypocritical streak in the British because it revealed a disdain for militarism, but allowed the British an empire:

> English literature, like other literatures, is full of battle-poems, but it is worth noticing that the ones that have won themselves a kind of popularity are always a tale of disasters and retreats. There is no poem about Trafalgar or Waterloo, for instance. Sir John Moore's army at Corunna, fighting a desperate rearguard action before escaping overseas (just like Dunkirk!) has more appeal than a brilliant victory. The most stirring battle-poem in English is about a brigade of cavalry which charged in the wrong direction.[15]

The celebration of these disasters became a way of interpreting them and then doing little about them other than to lionise them as examples of Britishness. Using this as a yardstick, it is possible to explain away many historical events, putting a gloss on British disasters. The death of Gordon at Khartoum is thus recast as an act of heroism. Gordon's contradiction of his orders and the failure of the government to send relief forces until it was far too late are therefore forgotten. Captain Oates's death in the expedition to the South Pole becomes a typically British quixotic gesture, not a desperate act by a man reduced to a pitiful wreck. The death of Captain Scott and chums in the same expedition has the hallowed aura of bravery against the odds. After all, why take only husky dogs like that tradesman Amundsen, get to the South Pole and back quickly and efficiently when you can take ponies that will drop dead almost immediately and then die yourself? The *Titanic* revealed how Englishmen and women die with stiff upper lips (of course, the image of the *Titanic* has changed considerably in recent years). Dunkirk and the Battle of Britain fit the legend too (why bother to have a well-equipped, large, modern army and air force at the start of the war when you can have jolly good, British-larks-in-a-boat-fun evacuating the remnants of an army and then leave the defence of the nation to a few dozen brave Brylcreem Boys?). Even the Falklands campaign can be seen in this light (why bother defending a far outpost correctly or sending the right diplomatic signals to a fascist power when you can cock it all up and be forced to send an expeditionary force halfway across the globe, thus stacking the odds against them?).

Tim Brooke-Taylor, in his light-hearted but none the less highly illuminating vignette on national character and culture, *Rule Britannia*, dedicated a chapter to 'Heroic Moments'. He noted:

> When it comes down to it, the British aren't honestly that fussed about winning. Better a gallant loser than an outright victor in most of our eyes, and if we do have to win, it has to be by the narrowest margin. What makes British heroism so impressive is the way we lose, going down with all guns blazing, fighting to the last man, rallying round the standard. These are the ideals and examples that raise a lump in every good British throat – and which were partially responsible for the loss of the Empire. But that's another story.
>
> Pluck any name from the roll-call of great British heroes and the chances are that he'll have made his name in some valiant, last-ditch stand or futile escapade, which concentrated public imagination and

distracted it from the general fiasco in which he was one small, heroic part. That's not to say that there aren't heroes that do win. But they've got to start as underdogs to score the full heroic tally.[16]

It is possible to read this view of national culture in a number of ways. It can be accepted as a good myth, something that is generally a beneficent part of the national fabric. It can be laughed at, but not thought too destructive. Or it can be violently opposed, condemned as invidious, as a way in which the traditional ruling classes have held power without ever being held responsible for their actions. It can also be condemned for holding the nation back, for stunting it and making it unable to accept change. Richardson certainly appeared to be making a protest at the passive acceptance of such disastrous events as the Charge of the Light Brigade and the resultant deflection from its true lessons. Ironically, Mrs Thatcher was later to express much the same opinion of certain national characteristics, thus creating a weird alliance with English football hooligans. The nasty atmosphere whipped up by newspapers like *The Sun* whenever England play 'traditional foes' such as Germany or France shows that English notions of sportsmanship and fair play have been discarded.

The Charge of the Light Brigade was hardly a new subject for cinema. It first hit the screens in 1903 and further silent versions appeared in 1912, 1914 and 1928; then in 1936 came the famed Warner Brothers version starring Errol Flynn. But the real catalyst for Richardson's interest in the Charge of the Light Brigade was Cecil Woodham-Smith's 1953 book, *The Reason Why*.[17] Three years earlier she had published an account of Florence Nightingale's life and work to tremendous acclaim. *The Reason Why* was also centred on the Crimean War and told the story of the Charge of the Light Brigade via the focus of the wildly fractious relationship between the brothers-in-law, and rival cavalry commanders, Lord Lucan and Lord Cardigan. *The Reason Why* was another great success and captivated Richardson. It also caught the imaginations of many others within the film world.

The screen rights to *The Reason Why* had been sold long before Richardson and Osborne turned their full attention to the topic. Michael Balcon, among others, had once been the owner, but by the 1960s the rights lay with Laurence Harvey, best known for his role as Joe Lampton in the film version of *Room at the Top* (1958). Osborne and Richardson wanted to avoid any clashes with Harvey and so set up a research department under John Mollo, a keen student of military history. To

avoid any infringement of Woodham-Smith's work, Mollo's brief was
to investigate the original sources, ensuring that any incident covered in
their project was well documented in other works and archives. John
Mollo therefore worked diligently, compiling a great deal of information
which he passed on to Osborne who was busy working on the script. It
was also the intention not to simply revise the famous 1936 Errol Flynn
film. Richardson had certainly seen this film as a child. By the time he
started on his own work he had a good knowledge of its sources, for he
noted in his autobiography that the Flynn film was largely based on
Alexander Kinglake's *Invasion of the Crimea*.[18]

Determined to make the film in the genuine location, Richardson
needed a lot of money. Luckily, he had the full backing of United Artists.
Hollywood was smiling on British film-makers and film companies at
this time, believing that Swinging London had its finger on the pulse.[19]
A movie combining a young cast with a good old-fashioned costume
drama appeared a dream team. Having gained United Artists' complete
trust, Osborne and Richardson felt responsible for using their big budget
wisely.

Osborne's script clearly caused problems for Richardson, though it
is unclear exactly how and why. In his autobiography Richardson was
tight-lipped, merely stating: 'It had many splendid and poetic things in
it – especially in its evocation of English society before the Crimean
War – but it still needed a lot of work.'[20] It was the start of a protracted
wrangle that would eventually lead to a major argument between Richardson and Osborne and their estrangement for many years.

To facilitate forward movement on the script, Richardson invited the
young writer Charles Wood to work on it, seemingly in tandem with
Osborne. Wood's introduction to the film is shrouded in mystery. He
told me that he knew about the project as he was working for Woodfall
on *The Knack*. John Osborne then asked him to take the job over. Wood
said: 'I have to say that I would not have taken the job if John hadn't
asked me himself.'[21] This is a slightly different version to the one given
by Richardson. It was a good choice: Wood's eccentric and comic turn
of mind gave the script power and energy, and as a national serviceman,
he had been in the 17/21st Lancers, a unit that had taken part in the
Charge of the Light Brigade. He recalled being told the story of the
charge by his superior officers, 'a ghastly mistake draped in a mantle of
heroism'. Not quite understanding the message of the story he asked a
fellow trooper what it was all about: '"All gets pissed Balaclava day", I
was assured ... and we did, come the day.'[22] These flippant and ironic

2. *Turkish cavalrymen made up the numbers in the dramatic charge sequence.*

remarks should not blind us to the fact that it gave Wood an excellent insight into the military mind and why ordinary soldiers followed their officers even in the most insane situations. He had also read *The Reason Why*, in addition to William Howard Russell's memoirs and Mrs Duberly's journals.[23] Such reading and experiences gave Wood a good grasp of the period and its background.

Wood claimed in a *Sight and Sound* interview that his role in the film came about only once the legal wrangle with Laurence Harvey began.[24] The argument exploded when Harvey managed to get hold of a copy of Osborne's script. He regarded it as a complete lifting from *The Reason Why* and therefore an infringement of the work he owned the rights to. He announced his intention to sue for plagiarism. Richardson and Osborne immediately engaged a QC to investigate the matter. When the QC reported back, the news was bad. As far as he could tell, Osborne's work was far too close to Woodham-Smith's. Though he had avoided the direct repetition of scenes from the book, 'he had helped himself liberally to stylistic phrases and descriptions'.[25]

In February 1967 a preliminary hearing went against Woodfall.

According to Richardson, the legal position was that Osborne was guilty of having used *The Reason Why*. Further, he was in breach of his scriptwriting contract with Woodfall and, most disturbingly, Woodfall was now in breach of its contract with United Artists. Osborne had left himself open to criminal prosecution. With such a juicy story in the air, it was not long before the press got hold of it. *The Sun* crowed '£2 million film may never be shown' and went on to describe the legal position.[26]

Wood claims he was brought in at about this time. He suspects that Richardson had already started planning an alternative script, but wanted to buy time with the lawyers. He therefore brought in a young, inexperienced writer and encouraged him to write a draft script that could be presented in court to confuse the lawyers who were expecting to see Osborne's work. Whatever the real motivation, Wood threw himself into the project:

> I duly produced three hundred pages or so of it, wildly surreal, anachronistic, savage, overwritten, pornographic, crammed with art student polemic, optimistically ironic, bitter about class and privilege; everything I felt about the British Empire, the British army, England under Queen Victoria and the first of the modern wars inspired by and based on Stephen Vincent Benet's 'John Brown's Body', Eisenstein's published screenplay of *Ivan the Terrible* and John Osborne's *Tom Jones*.[27]

Apparently, Richardson quite liked the script. Wood presented it to him while Richardson was eating breakfast, still in his pyjamas, and wearing a Crimean campaign medal. He presented Wood with one. But Richardson also pointed out his reservations: 'I don't think we can have Queen Victoria fucked by a bear, not even a very funny Russian bear, do you?'[28] He then sent Wood away to work on a new draft, while his original was used in the court case.

Richardson avoided this part of the story in his memoirs, referring only to the need to produce a solution that did not mean halting the production completely. United Artists agreed with Woodfall that the rights to *The Reason Why* had to be acquired and so a deal had to be made with Harvey. It is a mark of how important American investment was to the British film industry that Lord Goodman, a confidant of Prime Minister Harold Wilson, was appointed to act as a go-between. No one wanted the project to fall through. Eventually, Harvey was persuaded to make a deal but one of his conditions was a role in the film. Richardson racked his brains for a role Harvey could comfortably fill. He alighted on that of Prince Radziwill, a dandy Polish officer (ironically referring Harvey back to his Eastern European origins) attached to the British and French armies. This was not an ideal solution, for John Osborne himself had wanted to play this role. It led to the final collapse of Osborne and Richardson's relationship, which had been straining under the pressure of the legal wrangles. Osborne accused Richardson of betraying him and he absolutely refused to understand the position Richardson was in. Osborne stormed out of their partnership. All the Woodfall companies were eventually split and they never collaborated again. In a fit of pique Osborne wrote two vitriolic plays in which a self-pitying, arrogant, aloof film-maker alienates all around him: *Time Present* and *The Hotel in Amsterdam*. The project was under way again, but hardly in the brightest of circumstances.

However, Wood was at last free to use *The Reason Why* and he could take all he wanted from Osborne's original work. Richardson had wanted him to beef up the female roles, in particular that of Clarissa, a part he had in mind for Vanessa Redgrave. In the event, Wood claims that he mostly used Osborne's work for these scenes.[29] With shooting about to begin Wood accompanied the team and became a source of reference throughout.

Casting was less of a problem. Richardson could rely upon a team of good, young actors. Kevin Brownlow recalled that Richardson said 'half the job of directing is casting'.[30] David Hemmings and Vanessa Redgrave were cast as the young leads. Alan Dobie, Mark Burns, Corin Redgrave and Roger Mutton took the other young roles. T. P. McKenna was expertly cast as William Howard Russell and Peter Bowles and Jill Bennett brought great comedy and gusto to their roles of Captain and Mrs Duberly. The older roles were filled by an equally impressive array of talent, topped by John Gielgud as Lord Raglan and Trevor Howard as Lord Cardigan with Harry Andrews in the role of Lord Lucan, backed by Mark Dignam as General Airey and Norman Rossington as Sergeant Major Corbett. Originally, Richardson had wanted Rex Harrison for the part of Lord Lucan, but Harrison was already committed to other projects.[31] It is fascinating to consider how Harrison would have played the role and how he would have 'sparked' against Howard's Cardigan.

On the technical side, too, Richardson could rely on a very strong team, many of whom had worked together on other Woodfall projects. Charles Wood already knew David Watkin, the cinematographer, thanks to *The Knack*, and became close friends with John Mollo.[32] David Watkin's considerable expertise brought a quite remarkable period feel to

the photography. Watkin was a maverick talent and so was tempera-
mentally suited to Richardson. He had refused to undergo the usual
training and therefore had a long-standing feud with the unions. But his
work on Richard Lester's *The Knack* and on Richardson's *Mademoiselle*
had proved his skill. Kevin Brownlow, as editor, had a good historical
grasp of the subject and a great zeal for the project. Though he had
turned down Richardson's original offer, he became involved after he
had seen some rushes which greatly impressed him and learned that
Richardson was not seeing eye-to-eye with his original editor.[33] The skills
of Watkins and Brownlow, combined with the costumes of David Walker
and the brilliance of Lila de Nobili as the colour and period consultant,
resulted in a visual treat. De Nobili had worked for Visconti and Zeffirelli
and had a long track-record in theatre and opera. She worked closely
with David Watkin and John Mollo to ensure that the look of the film
was perfect. Watkin recalled her absolute dedication to her craft and her
willingness to work in close harmony with him.[34] Her eye for detail and
colour is obvious throughout the film and she played a large role in
creating the authenticity of its overall *impression*. For that is what the film
created, an impression of mid-Victorian Britain. A fascinating addition
to the team – but one that was by no means an afterthought – was
the young Canadian animator Richard Williams. Richardson wanted
Williams to supply short cartoons to fill in the larger narrative. According
to David Watkin, Williams got his chance after Richardson realised it
would be impossible to shoot a panorama shot of the transport ships at
sea.[35] Charles Wood told a different story: the second draft of the script
included linking scenes.[36] Williams took to his work with enthusiasm and
produced some of the most enduring images of the movie.

Richardson made no secret of the fact that he wanted to film on the
Crimean peninsula itself. At the height of the Cold War this was a neat
trick to pull off. Negotiations with the Russians proceeded only slowly,
and after a long wait they declined permission on the grounds that the
filming would take place too close to a military missile base. Woodfall
let it be known that the refusal was due to Russian sensitivity at having
lost the Crimean War. The *Daily Sketch* reported the final breakdown
in negotiations and noted that Herbert Wilcox had also been refused
permission to film in the area, though it is unclear which project this
referred to (probably his biopic of Florence Nightingale, *The Lady with
the Lamp*).[37]
     Woodfall turned to the other Black Sea state involved in the war –

Turkey. Turkey was one of the few countries that still kept a large cavalry force, intended to counteract Russian cavalry stationed in the border regions. Geographically it was well-suited, too, having many landscapes similar to those of the Crimea. Negotiations were opened between Woodfall and the Turkish government. Richardson noted that the American and French embassies in Turkey were only too ready to help him, whereas the British Foreign Office and diplomatic service were rarely of any great assistance. He repaid this alleged snub by refusing to cancel shooting on the Queen's birthday, thus preventing the cast and crew from attending the embassy party.

Dealing with the Turkish government proved to be an equally tricky business. The President of Turkey was the former head of the armed forces, with his former second-in-command replacing him at the top of the High Command. A delicate balance of power developed between the two. The President was anxious to show his authority over the armed forces, but at the same time the commander-in-chief was equally anxious to stress his powers. Both parties had to be kept onside during the talks, for the co-operation of both was vital. A deal was eventually brokered whereby the government supplied the cavalry but Woodfall agreed to pay for their up keep. Matters were helped by the fact that the commander of the cavalry became great friends with Richardson. Woodfall brought him to London and provided him with boxes of cigars and a quantity of saucy underwear for his girlfriend. Friendly co-operation seemed assured.

Once the deal was agreed, scouting began for appropriate locations. Two valleys about twenty miles from Ankara were thought suitable. But negotiations had to begin again, for the valleys were under the authority of two different villages and the co-operation of their councils was required. Woodfall wanted the villagers to agree not to plant any crops in the valleys and so had to come to an agreement about compensation. The villagers proved shrewd operators, forcing a deal in which they received about three times the amount they would have got for their crops. Even then the deal did not hold up properly, for by night the villagers destroyed the sets erected in the valleys, ploughed the fields to make them dangerous for the horses and caused numerous other nuisances.

In order to avoid any embarrassing situations, Richardson assembled the cast and crew on their arrival in May 1967. He made a speech telling everyone to abide by local customs and refrain from any sort of argument with the locals or the army. It was a tall order. Turkish soldiers

treated the villagers like dirt and so there was a running feud between
the two groups. In Ankara, one of the actors saw a young man and his
girlfriend throwing stones at frogs in a park pond. After remonstrating
with the man it transpired that he was one of the cavalry officers and
was deeply insulted by the actor's comments. The colonel of the regiment wanted Richardson to flog the actor to make an example of him.
Instead, much humble pie had to be consumed and grovelling apologies
made. An eccentric British stuntman and master of the horses tried to
train the cavalrymen in the art of screen fighting. It all went a bit too
far and Richardson was horrified to find that a grand rehearsal led to
some nasty injuries to the men and the need to destroy two horses.
Stories of squabbles had been getting back to the Turkish press and it
was claimed that ten soldiers had been killed on the production. Richardson took the opportunity to sack the stuntman and had to make more
apologies.

A constant worry was the appalling condition the Turkish soldiers
were kept in. Woodfall had followed the instructions of the government
in the making of accommodation for the troops and cavalrymen. Large
huts had been constructed which were promptly used for the horses,
while the men were left under canvas or in shacks. It was clear the
government cared little for the ordinary men and yet at one point some
4,000 Turkish troops were with the crew. According to Richardson, the
horses were donated by the Americans as part of an aid package. Further,
he claimed, they were old Hollywood mounts used in the Westerns![38] In
his memoirs Richardson noted that at no stage did they use a trip-wire
and no horses were hurt – though a couple did keel over and die from
old age. David Watkin is also adamant that every precaution was taken
with the horses.[39] However, Don Radovitch stated that the current
Connoisseur Video version of the film was released only after the now
illegal trip-wire scenes had been removed.[40]

With Richardson fighting off one problem after another the strained
atmosphere could easily have poisoned the whole shoot. John Gielgud
certainly did not enjoy himself. Early on in the shooting he was thrown
from his horse which shook his confidence badly. Richardson was forced
to have him flanked by two other riders in all subsequent shots so they
could keep a close eye on the animal. Gielgud wrote in his memoirs:
'The Turks were very tough with us, did not care for us at all and made
things as difficult as they could for Tony Richardson.'[41] However, it is
a tribute to Richardson that Gielgud was also able to state that *The
Charge of the Light Brigade* was the first film in which he was treated

like a proper actor and his craft was respected.[42] Trevor Howard also found the Turks a rough lot, and he noted, 'the Turks didn't really seem to like us too much and made life difficult for everyone'.[43] At least Richardson did not have to worry about Howard's legendary drinking, for his biographer claimed Howard hardly touched a drop throughout the shooting in Turkey, was popular with the crew with whom he shared only the odd drink and was deeply appreciative of the chance to work with Gielgud.[44] Watkin supports this interpretation and remembers Howard's dedication to the job.[45]

The big battle scenes were the most difficult problems to solve. George Lellis argued in *Sight and Sound* that Richardson had 'a lousy sense of landscape ... Put him outdoors, amid hills, terrain and geography, with people on horses, saying little and doing much, and the movie just doesn't know what to do.'[46] This is nonsense. One of the most impressive aspects of the movie is Richardson's handling of grand panoramas and the movement of the troops across a dramatic landscape.

Somehow Richardson managed to get 4,000 Turkish soldiers into period uniforms (Mollo's research was invaluable) and shot a powerful Battle of the Alma sequence, in which the British army scales the cliffs to attack the Russian positions. At one point smoke drifts across the camera revealing glimpses of the cliffs and the assaulting infantry. A marvellous visual spectacle is presented. David Watkin revealed that the 'flag' protecting the camera from the sun slipped at just the wrong moment. However, he did not realise it until he was viewing the rushes with Richardson. He advised Richardson that they were unlikely to be able to get the smoke to drift in quite the same way, or catch the sun in quite the same position again. Richardson therefore decided to go with it.[47] Sharp-eyed viewers will be able to spot the slight smudge in the left-hand corner of the shot, the tell-tale sign of the slipped flag. Perhaps even more impressive was the landing at Calamita Bay. For this Richardson assembled a series of barges on the Bosporus. Men, guns and horses were loaded on to the barges and had to be rowed ashore. On the morning of the shoot the temperamental waters of the Bosporus proved a bit lively. Richardson found that many of the soldiers were hopelessly seasick. Needing numbers to convey the impressiveness of the original landing, he had the crew prop up as many sick soldiers as they could. The scene on the screen is an amazing one as men, animals and gear pile off barges and on to the beach.

Of course the centrepiece was the actual Charge of the Light Brigade itself, but Richardson also filmed a huge charge of the Heavy Brigade

as well (the event that immediately preceded the Light Brigade action)
and the Russian storming of the British forts. One of the criticisms later
thrown at the film is that the final charge is unimpressive given its long
build-up. It has been said that Richardson intended a charge sequence
involving far more horsemen, but was blocked by the Turkish government recalling the cavalry at the last minute. Richardson does not
mention this story but Munn, Howard's biographer does. Munn claimed
that only about sixty men were available on the day of shooting. He
added: 'Had he been able to shoot the charge and the battle with the
Turkish army, as he did the thundering battles that precede the charge,
he would have turned out an undisputed masterpiece.'[48] But neither
Kevin Brownlow nor David Watkin has mentioned this story to me and
I have found no other source for it. I must admit to being completely
unaware of any sense of a small-scale final charge until I read this and
similar criticisms. My own understanding of the scene was that it was
naturally smaller than the Alma scenes because far fewer men were
involved. I also thought that Richardson wanted us to feel the same
sense of smallness and utter isolation as those men in that huge valley,
a valley that must have suddenly felt even bigger and even more open
once they started to move along it, unsupported by infantry or their
own artillery. The real problem probably lies in the way the individual
watches the film; if one is expecting a traditional grand war epic finale,
then the charge probably does look like a damp squib. However, it was
partly inspired by some grand epics. The cavalry charge from Raymond
Bernard's *The Chess Player* was shown to Richardson by Kevin Brownlow. Brownlow also recorded watching sequences from *Quiet Flows the
Don* with Richardson and John Mollo. 'There was a shout from the
back. "That's what we want". I thought he was nuts.'[49]

Once back in England, the cast and crew felt a huge sense of relief.
Aided by a good summer, Watkin's photography, combined with de
Nobile's vision, created a lush Pre-Raphaelite world. When the eye is
not inspired by Rossetti-like canvases then the photographs of Julia
Margaret Cameron and David Octavius Hill come to mind.

Post-production work then began in earnest. Richard Williams had
been busy on the animations for well over two years, but such was the
extreme skill and patience required to create them that sequences were
being added right up to the day of the première itself.

Editing was hardly a subtle process. By his own admission Richardson
was 'a fanatical cutter'.[50] Brownlow agreed, saying: 'He kept cutting ...
he didn't have much editorial sense.'[51] According to Brownlow, Richard-

son's lack of editorial sense also reflected a lack of confidence in his own skills as a director. The almost indiscriminate desire to cut was motivated by his fear that what he had shot had no value. One of the first incisions was the deliberate removal of Laurence Harvey. The cause of so much trouble was famously consigned to the merciless cutting-room floor. One of Harvey's scenes never even made it on to film. According to Watkin, Richardson told him not to load the camera during one of his rare appearances.[52] The *Daily Mail* picked up on this, reproduced a portrait photograph of Harvey in costume and ran the headline: 'The most expensive face on the cutting room floor'.[53] Richardson cut huge sections, including the large-scale charge of the Heavy Brigade. Kevin Brownlow, revealing his historian's mind, wanted to keep every scene and reshape it into a special four-and-a-half-hour version. Tragically, the project was never instigated and the fragments have now been lost. One can only bemoan the loss of so much material and wonder at what might have been.

In order to ensure a perfect première, Richardson introduced his dubbing engineer, Gerry Humphreys, to the team at the Odeon, Leicester Square. Humphreys rehearsed the soundtrack on their equipment, adjusting and fine-tuning the levels to Richardson's direction. On the opening night when the film started rolling it very quickly became evident that the sound was at a much lower level than had been rehearsed. Humphreys rushed off to the projection booth to ask what was happening. The projectionist explained that Sir John Davis, owner of the Rank circuit, was in attendance and he refused to allow the sound beyond a certain level whenever he was in the audience. 'But it's Mr Richardson's film,' protested Humphreys. 'It may be Mr Richardson's film,' replied the projectionist, 'but it's Sir John's theatre.'[54]

TWO
The Narrative

The major problem in analysing the plot of *The Charge of the Light Brigade* is establishing a viewpoint from which to examine the film. Did Richardson create a kitchen sink drama in period costume? Was it a variation on *Tom Jones*? Was it a historical war epic? Was it an allegory of his own time? Or was it all four? The problem of categorising the film has stumped many commentators and critics. It seems to me that it is best to see it as a film without a definite catalogue label.

What one notices immediately about the film is the interest in sex and sexuality. The roles of the sexes were of concern to both Victorians and the youth of the 1960s. Wood reflected the increased questioning of gender roles by exploring the perceptions of the Victorians. It is implied that the mid-Victorian period was actually a time of flux and some contradiction, not unlike the '60s.

Masculinity is portrayed as a somewhat ambiguous concept. War and sex certainly seem to be intimately connected. Andy Medhurst has noted that 'the film is full of men for whom war holds an erotic charge'.[1] The young Captain Nolan embodies this as much as his arch-enemy Lord Cardigan.[2] Nolan's entire *raison d'être* is to fight and feel its glorious, exhilarating power. Clarissa seems to detect this streak of sensual addiction in him, asking him whether soldiers should have wives. He carefully excludes himself by saying his friend William should, and leaves it at that. However, this does not mean the thought of fighting fulfils him so much he has no sexual desire. Rather, it is that the two are intimately connected and stimulate each other, but ultimately war is his real mistress. Mrs Duberly asks Nolan whether war is terrible. He replies: 'It is *the stuff*. It is the stuff we are all waiting for.' Later Clarissa is forced to concede that war and violence may be innate qualities of men, for she reflects, 'Perhaps there is no other life for a man ... how sad.' Nolan feels it is his mission to fight, to fight with great ferocity but with great skill and efficiency too.

Lord Cardigan shows a similar streak. He equates sex with violence, but does not have Nolan's sense of reforming zeal or mission. For him the whole job of soldiering is one big orgy-cum-adventure that enhances his aristocratic demeanour and masculine bearing. The film opens with Cardigan reviewing his cavalry regiment; we hear him in voiceover saying, 'If they can't fornicate, they can't fight.' Sexual prowess is seen to be the inspiration and necessary prerequisite for the true masculinity of the battlefield.

However, there is an irony in the construction of masculinity, for it is also based upon a seemingly feminine preoccupation with looks and appearance. One of the great strengths of the film is its stunning ward-robe, with the most glorious costumes being the painstakingly researched authentic military uniforms. The cavalry officers and men are bedecked in flamboyant uniforms, miles of gold braid and frogging, cherry-red breeches, high leather boots, beautiful shakos and other headgear. Lord Cardigan calls his red-breeched men his 'cherrybums' which he keeps 'tight' and spends 'ten thousand a year out of me own pocket ... to clothe 'em'. Mrs Duberly calls the men Lord Cardigan's 'beautiful soldiers'. Cardigan is aroused by the sight of his men dressed according to his baroque tastes. He tells his friend, a fat squire: 'Had me cherry-bums out this morning, always makes me feel randified.'

Femininity is also presented in an ambiguous way. Clarissa is certainly the essence of an affectionate woman, prepared to defer to the wisdom of the men who surround her. Redgrave plays the role with a great deal of affecting pathos and empathy. Clarissa is seen to be a loving and gentle person. An all-pervading atmosphere of romance fills her ap-pearances on the screen. Such an atmosphere is very much aided by making her a creature of the countryside. We see her sitting in her rural home, or walking in her garden which is a mixture of formal flowerbeds and romantic wildernesses, or punting on deep green, reedy rivers. The rich golds, browns, russets and greens of her surroundings make her a person in sympathy with nature. They also make her seem like the heroine of a Pre-Raphaelite painting.

A much more raucous femininity is seen in the army wives who live in barracks with their menfolk. They are matronly and jolly, stereotypes of rumbustious washer-women and the maids of all work that were so much a part of military and naval life. Their matronliness is combined with a certain earthy sexual knowledge. They are frequently seen in their underwear while scrubbing away at the clothes. They seem to know the men are looking at them and have their own ripostes to any

innuendo thrown their way. They take a great delight in gently goading
Rupert Codrington, the handsome, innocent young officer. In these
scenes Richardson clearly draws on the world of bawdy sexual delights
he had already created in *Tom Jones*. However, they are still performing
a traditional feminine role, that of the comic serving maid and camp
follower. One in six army wives were allowed to follow their husbands
to the Crimea in order to perform a similar array of ancillary roles. The
film later shows them in camp, sharing the same hardships as their
menfolk.

By contrast, the film also shows the women who were left behind –
Clarissa among them. The departure scene reveals the stereotypical
devoted females, kissing their loved ones goodbye, their faces filled with
anxiety, concern and love. Richardson's shots of the soldiers clambering
aboard the troopship with their wives and sweethearts packing the gang-
planks and clasping the bulwarks and rigging are extremely powerful. It
is also an almost exact replica of Henry Nelson O'Neil's painting of
troops leaving to suppress the Indian Mutiny, *Eastward Ho!* By re-
creating scenes from Victorian paintings and illustrations, Richardson
helps to give the film a period authenticity and emotional intensity.

But the film never sympathises too much with overtly patronising or
traditional views of women and their historically allotted roles. Lord
Raglan's understanding of women is used to comic effect. When Mrs
Duberly asks him to explain the unfolding battle of Balaclava, he treats
her like a child. Such behaviour is clearly in accordance with his own
concept of the polite and correct way to deal with a woman. He tells
her: 'Young ladies should concern themselves with things that are pretty.
England is pretty. Babies are pretty. Some table linen can be very pretty
… Find a pretty flower and press it in your housebook and watch the
pretty valley.'

The act of sex itself is important to the film, as it was to the time in
which it was made. Victorian sexual morality, a prudish sexual morality
that had dominated Britain for a long time, was under heavy assault and
scrutiny in the 1960s. Richardson and Wood show up Victorian attitudes
as hypocritical and obstructive to true emotions. Nowhere is this more
crudely and effectively shown than in the portrayal of the sex lives of
the upper classes. The aristocratic ethos which had claimed that its right
to rule was based upon superiority in every field, including that of
innate virtue (always a veneer designed to cover a multitude of sins), is
blown sky high by the film. Aristocratic sexual morality is seen to be
degenerate and crude. Cardigan is a boorish oaf who enjoys sating his

base desires. When a society lady approaches him at a ball he turns his back on her. For once he does not actually desire a woman, but he enjoys his friend's crude, sexual joke at her expense: 'They tell me her pitcher has been too often to the well.'[3] Instead, Cardigan is far more interested in seducing the wife of one of his officers, Mrs Duberly. Mrs Duberly encourages his attentions and notes that her husband 'says I must stop looking at Lord Cardigan as if I want to be ridden by him. Duberly says he has left his wife and has a most notorious, casual way with women. Immoral and licentious ... Is he not the very picture of the finest Englishman?' The women here are no mere playthings of men but actively encourage the process of seduction and infidelity.

As Cardigan comes to take more notice of Mrs Duberly, Richardson and Wood use it as a chance to inject more satirical and bawdy comedy. Cardigan invites her to dine on his yacht and finally gets her alone. As they undress both reveal corsets. Cardigan is not the young stud he so desperately wants to appear but a fat, ageing lothario. This does not stop Mrs Duberly from comically cooing: 'You have the mane of a lion.' Pushing her over Cardigan replies: 'I like saddles, get on your back ... It is by no means a bad thing when getting onto a strange horse for the first time to give the middle of the saddle three or four hard bangs with the flat of the hand.' He then proceeds to slap her bottom. The whole scene is played for grotesque comedy. Cardigan clearly has no respect for her other than as a sex object. By the same token Mrs Duberly is not bothered because she has an image of Cardigan as a great, virile man, which, by comparison with her husband, he is. Once again the scent of *Tom Jones* is palpable.

This lampooning of Victorian sexual morality is set against a balancing infidelity, one that is presented very differently. Nolan's affair with Clarissa is presented as a thing of great pathos. As Nolan sees more of his best friend's new wife, it becomes more and more obvious that there is a strong attraction between them. Richardson used the camera to create a loving homage to his wife, but menacing trumpets heard in John Addison's score interrupt these otherwise idyllic scenes. When Nolan and Clarissa make love it is presented as just that, an act of love between two passionate young people. It has none of the pantomime humour of Cardigan's seduction of Mrs Duberly. The anguish of Clarissa at her infidelity is palpable, especially when she finds she is pregnant. We sympathise with her infidelity because she is torn by a genuine moral dilemma. She loves her husband and yet loves Nolan too. Perhaps this theme is meant to question the value of marriage as an institution. Does marriage create more problems than it solves? Perhaps in a society which did not demand absolute fidelity it would be possible to love more freely and this would take away the risk of unintended hurt? If this was indeed the message, it seems to be one very much of its time.

Such a sympathetic portrayal of infidelity is connected with the age of the protagonists. Cardigan is an old man displaying all the traits of an older, less worthy age. The young, on the other hand, are glorious and glamorous crusaders for change and reform. But it is not presented as a simple parable of youth, always right and the old always wrong, as we would perhaps expect from a typical '60s film. The character of Nolan is the most ambiguous and intriguing. He bears a certain resemblance to Jimmy Porter. Both men are restless and feel trapped by the conventions made by older men, both long for a cause in which to lose themselves. Nolan is an angry young man, but not the sort of angry young man so beloved of the radical fringe of '60s youth. No anti-war protests come from Nolan; instead he is desperate to fight and to reform the army. Believing Britain to be strangled by the old, he seeks to establish the supremacy of youth and the new. He highlights the foolishness of beating discipline into horses by using, in his term, 'gentleness'. In one scene we see him win over a horse that has been startled by a whipping. He climbs on and we hear him chant softly his mantra 'gently, gently', slowly calming the horse. Then he reprimands his brother officer, 'horses are taught not by harshness but by gentleness'.[4] After yet another quarrel with Cardigan he dreams that:

> one day there will be an army where troopers need not be forced to fight by floggings and hard brains. An army, a Christian army that fights because it is paid well to fight, and fights well because its women and children are cared for. An army that is efficient and of a professional feather. I must fight for such an army. That army will be the first of the modern wars and the last of the gallant.

Yet when he is in the Crimea, he comes across a group of dishevelled British soldiers who are cooking their breakfast. Without questioning their condition he takes their food and eats it in front of the starving men. Galloping off across the landscape with Morris he is thrilled and vibrant, he is clearly exhilarated by war. The scene cuts back to the poor soldiers. Corbett, an ordinary trooper, looks at his empty pan and mutters, 'Some of these officers have got bloody little pride at times.' Here we start to see the contradictions in Nolan's character. His cause is to create Christian mercenaries. He wants to look after women and children, but also to create an instrument that brings so much misery to women and children. It is a glorious cause, but will wipe away the last remnants of ancient chivalry by ushering in the modern. When the fighting starts, he is frustrated that it is the same old gang running affairs in the same old way. Exasperated, he tells Morris he had 'such high hopes of this war'. Morris replies he must be patient. This sparks Nolan to greater passion:

> No, I am not patient. I will not be patient, to the noble amateurs who are so sick of their soldiering they would go home under the ridiculous supposition that war is an aid to civilisation. War is destruction, William, not possession. It is standing booty over dead soldiers and their wives. The solution to war is that it is best fought and when fought it is best fought to the death.

For the man who seems to be an advocate of rational progress and improvement this appears like an incitement to naked savagery. However, it also seems like the truth, for rules to war do appear to be a contradiction and are, perhaps, an obstacle to its abolition. Nolan is a complex character indeed. Clarissa sums it up when she tells him, 'There is some madness in you, which has affected us all.'

But the point about youth in the film is that they, at least, have a sense of devotion and dedication, no matter how confused or contradictory it may seem. By contrast, the old men are either ridiculous, eccentric, argumentative, self-seeking, pompous or immoral, or a mixture of the lot. Cardigan is the symbol of the worst aspects of the old men. His ridiculous conceit and self-righteousness become even more accentuated once he finds he has to serve under his brother-in-law, Lord Lucan. From the moment war is declared the two men resurrect what is clearly a long-running feud. Raglan, as overall commander, seems more preoccupied in keeping the peace between the two parties than in fighting the enemy. A streak of black comedy runs through the relationship between the older men. On the one hand it is a farce; on the other it is obscene that such men should have power over the fate of the men under their commands. The satirical edge shows the spirit of the times and is not too far from the pages of *Private Eye* and the lampoons of the television show, *That was the Week that was*.

Lord Raglan is the most overtly comic character among the older men. He is reminiscent of satirical presentations of Harold Macmillan in the 1960s. When war looms, Raglan gathers his fellow senior officers in his office and talks to them of the plight of Turkey. General Airey remarks that Turkey is the sick man of Europe. Raglan looks pained and says he prefers to think of Turkey as a poor defenceless maiden who is looking desperately to the gentlemen of Britain to defend her from the awful Russian bear. Such a quaint, though charming, view is clearly meant to show us how detached Raglan is from the realities of the situation. This sense of detachment increases once the army arrives in the Crimea. Lucan brings a Russian deserter to Raglan, stating that the man is prepared to inform them of the Russian preparations. Raglan is disgusted by such behaviour. He says he will not dishonour himself by dealing with spies and reminds the young man of how ashamed his mother would be if she witnessed such dishonest behaviour.

The comic effect of such scenes is greatly increased by Wood's skilful use of language. He created a superb idiom by using the language of Carlyle, Thackeray and contemporary memoirs. He noted: 'Once you find a language for the characters to speak fitting the mood and aim of the film the rest seems to follow, though it wasn't easy to get actors to speak it properly at first.'[5] Cardigan uses the glorious anachronism 'wot': 'I do not propose to recount my life in any detail wot is wot/ No damn business of anyone wot is wot/ I am Lord Cardigan that is wot.' It is very hard not to think of T. E. Brown's contemporary ditty: 'a garden is a lovesome thing, God wot!' Many of the other officers are given comic inflexions to their speech. Captains Duberly and Featherstone-haugh cannot pronounce 'r'. We therefore hear lines such as, 'It was all a dweadful bore, the cavalwy was not used', and 'He should eat gwass like a wabbit'. There is much use of 'me', instead of 'my', and 'aint' instead of 'isn't', all of which are delivered by the otherwise high-bred officers. One of the officers, given the deliberately comic name Mogg, is lower class and desperate to prove himself a gentleman. He attempts to do this by adding, and dropping, aitches in the wrong places: 'There is not such things as a wobbly hofficer. What you sergeants will never seem to understand is the 'eavy state of responsibility that an hofficer is in. They worry, they 'ardly never wobble.' This kind of stylised language is very close to that of Squire Jorrocks, the comic Cockney grocer who became Master of Fox Hounds in R. M. Surtees' contemporary stories. Of course, this language and forms of address are seen most comically and most forcefully in the references to sex. When young Codrington is forced to eat lettuce as a punishment for not being able to control his horse, Cardigan tells him, 'Perhaps it'll put some sap in your pizzle.' Rather crude allusions are wrapped up in baroque and bawdy phrases that seem outlandish, comic and antique. The insults traded between Cardigan and Lucan are of this nature. Cardigan calls Lucan a 'stewstick' and a 'poltroon', in reply Lucan calls him a 'bumroll'. This exchange is wound up on the glorious line from Cardigan: 'Draw your horse from round your ears and take your head out of his arse.'

The language and idiom are fascinating for the way in which they dramatically heighten the sense of period and accuracy. Further, it is the proof of L. P. Hartley's words: the past truly is a foreign country. However, what the film seeks to question is just how differently they did things there as compared with the mid-1960s. The genius of the film lies in its ability to be a contemporary parable while retaining an absolutely authentic air of 1854.

Wood accompanied the team on the location work in order to help with the correct delivery of the lines. He recalled:

> The whole point of me being around during the shooting was so that I could help the actors to get their tongues round the (to them) strange syntax but after a while they didn't need any help and could indeed render anything into what became known as Woodery Pokery. The younger actors at first tried to colloquialise their speeches but Tony wouldn't allow that and I know they found difficulties. The only person not to have any trouble at all was Gielgud and I know that he helped some of the actors a great deal by simply reading it to them. From the moment that the 'language' was accepted everybody did their best to keep to it and I think it helped them to get into the rhythm of the thing.[6]

The wider historical framework of the film is established by Richard Williams's animated sequences. These excellently conceived and executed interludes provide the viewer with a barrage of different images, some comic and grotesque, some dramatic, some documentary. They never bewilder, they are easy to follow and are fascinating and entertaining in themselves. Williams drew on the contemporary engravings of the *Illustrated London News* and *Punch* for his sources and inspiration, thus giving his work added authenticity and vivacity. The initial credit sequence shows Britain in mid-century, a time when it had an undisputed lead in industry and technology had given it supremacy in the world. We see scenes from mines, factories and forges. We see bathing-machines and pleasure gardens and gentlemen in tight trousers and stove-pipe hats accompanying ladies and children. The two halves of Britain are therefore shown. The Crystal Palace arises, hinting at Britain's industrial supremacy and sense of social and racial superiority. This sense is reinforced by the vision of the various subject peoples of the empire paying homage to Queen Victoria. In a very effective, succinct and powerful way, the entire context of the film is established.

The cartoons and animations also hint at the film's element of hyper-reality and grotesque exaggeration. In one sequence, we see Russia caricatured in its usual nineteenth-century form as the great bear, which then chases a scared turkey. The British lion, which has been lying asleep, is roused, pulls on its policeman's helmet and sets off to help. Later Turkey is transformed into a damsel, swooning at the sight of the bear. Such an image reinforces Raglan's comments about Britain's self-perceived role in the war. The British lion is seen in Union flag overalls standing alongside the French cockerel. Bulldogs wearing the John Bull garb suddenly join them. The bulldogs attack the Russian bear and bring him down. France here seems to be a happy spectator, allegedly involved in the fighting but content to let Britain quite literally carry the lion's share. But in this ironic atmosphere the lion's share of the struggle is not presented as something to be proud of. Rather, it seems that Britain was too stupid to realise it was carrying the war alone.

The war fever of the time is also hinted at in Williams's animations. We see grotesque characters – very similar to the illustrations Tenniel executed for Dickens's works – mouth 'War, war, war, war'. Such a spirit did mark Britain in 1854, and the use of animation conveys it in a far more potent way than any ordinary reconstruction, for everything appears to have an immediacy and authority. The use of such an ex-aggerated and baroque technique gives the piece a greater sense of historical authenticity, invoking the atmosphere of the time.

The voyage to the Crimea is dealt with in the third sequence. The animation turns the rock of Gibraltar into a lion pointing across to the far side of the Mediterranean. Sailors climb the rigging of great ships and 'Rule Britannia' is heard. Once in Constantinople, hideous cari-catures of the various commanders are used. They clearly owe much to the mid-Victorian cartoons of Mr Punch. They are all red-faced, none more so than Cardigan, implying that all the commanders were rather gouty, apoplectic old men.

The final sequence deals with the period during which it was pre-maturely announced that Sebastapol had fallen. Being a moment of sanguine overconfidence, Williams portrays it most ironically. Victoria and Albert are seen as ballet dancers, romantically celebrating victory. John Bull pulls the strings of a tsar puppet. The tsar puts his head in the lion's mouth and promptly has it bitten off. Fireworks announce 'The

3. *Tony Richardson provides guidance to Vanessa Redgrave and Mark Burns for the wedding scene.*

Fall of Sebastopol', with that a cannon is heard and we are returned to the trenches outside the fortress, with the comment 'Fallen, me arse' from William Howard Russell, correspondent of *The Times*.

The Richard Williams animations certainly stand out. They are in some ways apart from the film, but they are not separate from it. Rather, they are integral to the overall texture and to an understanding of it. They do not detract from the 'reality' of the film because it is deliberately stylised, bringing us closer to the actual spirit of the time and of the 1960s.

A painstaking attention to detail ensured that the film established the right period feel, even if it is highly coloured by a 1960s understanding of how the period felt. At the start of the film Clarissa's wedding is a model of Victorian rural attitudes. Peasants in smocks wait eagerly for the distribution of cash by the happy couple. At the wedding reception popular songs are played on the upright piano. Ever since Mr Pooter's diary first appeared in 1892 we have known that an upright piano is a symbol of Victorian bourgeois responsibility. Interestingly, the colourful gaiety of the wedding scene cuts to an urban backstreet. From brightness we are plunged into deep greys, blacks and awful, sickly-looking tan and beige colours. Into this dull, depressing, Doré-like scene strolls a gorgeous uniform; it is a recruiting sergeant from the hussars. Richardson's clever use of cutting between incongruous scenes is shown when he reverses the process. We switch from the bawdy, raucous barracks room to the colour and swirl of a high society ball. A world of two, very firmly divided halves is created, between the haves and the have nots. Richard Williams does much the same in the opening animation sequence. For Richardson the common linking element between rich and poor is their earthy interest in sex.

Life in the Victorian army is portrayed with an eye to detail and some old clichés are repeated. New recruits are lured in by the promise of adventure, status and glory, but as soon as they are marched into the barracks, having 'taken the Queen's shilling', they are bawled at by the sergeant. They are referred to as 'scum'. This is meant to remind us of the Duke of Wellington's dictum that the army was made up of 'the scum of the earth, enlisted mainly for drink and rape'.

A very similar scene was later used in Richard Attenborough's anti-war, ironic parody *Oh! What a Lovely War* (1969) in which Maggie Smith appears as glamorous actress luring young men to the colours, backed by the strapping figure of Robert Shaw in uniform. No sooner do the young men prance on stage than they are marched off to Shaw's yelling and cursing. The 1960s' debunking of all military adventures is strongly reflected in both movies.

In the barracks the men are washed thoroughly and then yelled at some more. The need to wash the men not only shows how filthy they were in civilian life and how the army demands cleanliness as part of its regime of discipline, but also perhaps gives a sense of the ambiguous 'femininity' of soldiers in gorgeous, dandy uniforms. Such is the ignorance of the new recruits that they have to be taught their right leg from their left. Whenever Sergeant Corbett is shown dealing with the men, the camera takes a slight upwards gaze, showing that the ordinary troopers feel small in the presence of authority even though some of them are clearly taller than Corbett. We are also told that many of them have rickets, they are 'wobbly boned'. Having faced a barrage of abuse and orders, army life is given a flip-side; we also see how many women and children lived in a Victorian barracks, at least allowing the families to remain together.

For the officer army life is portrayed as one long round of trotting about on horses, lounging in the mess, playing puerile tricks and sumptuous dining. Our first introduction to the cavalry mess sets the scene for the rest of film. We see a grand Palladian-style façade, fronted by a gravel drive. Sunlight streams down, two officers are playing with a small ball, some others are lounging in wicker seats reading magazines or smoking cigars, others lie stretched out on the baluster. Over this idyllic, lovely vision we hear Nolan's voice: 'There is no place happier than a cavalry mess. If one is a stupid, inconsiderate and lazy fellow one can fit as a round peg in a snug round hole. At times I'm so pent-up with anger I could bang their noddles together till their doodles drop off.' Nolan's introduction sets up what kind of man he is and what kind of army he is in. The language he uses is, once again, of a highly stylised kind.

Nolan is presented as a threat to a hidebound, traditional army. His insistence on professionalism and study make him an outsider in an aristocratic club where such an attitude ill becomes a gentleman. Both Cardigan and Raglan take an immediate dislike to him for just that reason. An aristocratic understanding of the army demands that officers be natural, instinctive soldiers. They do not need to study the art of war, for it is in their blood. To Cardigan and Raglan, Nolan is nothing more than that most hideous of things – a tradesman. For Raglan, only the aristocracy can defend Britain; a wisdom he has learned from his mentor, the Duke of Wellington. 'He was surely right that when there is danger, it is the persons with a stake in the country, land, position and wealth that are best able to defend it.' Later Raglan condemns Nolan as a man that 'knows his job too well', explaining: 'That young man Nolan, I don't really like him, he rides too well. But he has no heart. It will be a sad day, Airey, when England has her armies officered by men who know too well what they are doing. It smacks of murder!'

Cardigan is very suspicious of Nolan's Indian army service. Woodham-Smith's book pointed out the jealousy of Indian army officers, for they had often seen active service, fighting on the North-West Frontier and against other enemies of the Raj. They therefore had a superiority over home service officers. Cardigan never misses an opportunity to disparage Nolan's Indian career or his Indian servant. 'Black savage' and 'black rogue' are just two of the insults Cardigan hurls at the servant, while Nolan himself is called 'an Indian wretch' and an 'impertinent Indian dog'. It is clear that Raglan's and Cardigan's preferred form of army is one that pays no attention to meritocracy or genuine professionalism. All advancement is achieved by purchase, or by knowing men in high places. Cornet Codrington reminds Raglan that his father had once served with him. Raglan remembers the incident and remarks, 'Yes, I did and I didn't like him. Don't look to me for advancement.' It is a theme often referred to in 1960s movies about the Victorian British establishment, and was linked to the contemporary attack on the 'old school tie'. In *Zulu*, Lieutenant Bromhead tells Lieutenant Chard his father had been at Waterloo and his grandfather had been with Wolfe at Quebec. Chard, the outsider, understands the implication exactly, Bromhead expects command of Rorke's Drift as a natural right. Attenborough also highlighted such themes in *Oh! What a Lovely War*. General Haig is said to owe his position to the Duke of Cambridge, a friend of the family, for he had failed his Staff College entrance examination.

Mogg, the 'Jorrocks officer', has no connections, nor has Duberly, and neither has much money. They also appear to be singularly talentless and are desperate for a war in which to get themselves noticed and so advance higher up the ranks. Duberly has little chance of that, however, for he is the paymaster officer and so hardly has a glamorous role. Cardigan has absolute contempt for a necessary, executive, but nonactive role and during a ferocious outburst yells: 'Officer! Officer! You're a paymaster, Duberly, that ain't a rank it's a trade.' Tradesman, the worst insult an aristocrat could think of.

The feud between Nolan, the symbol of youth, energy and professionalism, and Cardigan, symbol of reaction, age and intransigence, explodes in a mess room argument. Cardigan orders that only champagne can be drunk in the mess, but when Nolan orders a bottle of Moselle, which he does not decant, Cardigan takes the bottle to be cheap porter beer, thus lowering the esteem of his officers. He does not allow Nolan to explain and a furious row erupts. A theatre audience then ruin Cardigan's visit by chanting 'black bottle' as soon as he appears. Richardson and his team clearly enjoyed creating these scenes. Richardson took the chance to send up the famous performances of the great Victorian actor, Charles Kean, playing his favourite role of Macbeth. Sir Donald Wolfit is perfectly cast in the cameo, strutting around the Drury Lane stage, performing in a wildly over the top production of the Scottish play, while the audience boos and hisses the arrival of Cardigan.[7] (In order to give this scene an even greater period feel, Watkin had explored the possibility of lighting by limelight. However, it proved too technically difficult and he reluctantly abandoned the idea.)[8]

It is not just in the vendetta against Nolan that Cardigan shows up the hypocrisy and emptiness of his aristocratic values. Paranoid about Nolan's actions, he requests Sergeant-Major Corbett to spy on Nolan and report back all conversations. Corbett is presented as an excellent career soldier who has avoided drink, the great vice of Victorian soldiers, and has dedicated himself to the army. Corbett refuses to take part in this dishonourable job.[9] Without a second thought, without a hint of compunction, Cardigan tells him he is ruined, that his years of service are of no account and that he might as well shoot himself. In the next scene we see a drunken Corbett collapse on duty. Cardigan and his chums are looking on and they laugh at the pathetic spectacle. It then cuts to a church parade in the main equestrian exercise hall. The troopers are lined up on one side and visitors on the other. They sing hymns and the visitors appear happy. The viewer is aware of the codes of the film by now and there is a knowledge that such a scene must be followed by an ironic statement. Sure enough, the scene then cuts to show the men lined up to watch the flogging of Corbett for being drunk on duty.[10] Young Codrington passes out at the sight. Nolan remarks to Mogg that such punishments do not create a better army. Mogg asks: 'Would you have them fight for money or hideas that would be hunchristian?'

The army is not just inefficient, it also labours under the weight of history and is loath to alter what it believes is a successful formula. The main spirit of the army is the long dead Duke of Wellington. Wellington's image is everywhere in the film, reflecting not only his genuine historical legacy to mid-Victorian Britain, but also the 1960s fad for debunking great, dead white men. Raglan is always deferring to the memory of Wellington. Throughout the film he asks himself what the duke would have done.[11] Raglan cannot escape him and his office is dominated by a bust and portrait of the duke. It is, of course, the tragedy of the old men that they are preparing for the last war they fought, rather than a new one. As the old men gather at a ball, they discuss their previous experiences. General Browning remembers, 'I danced as a boy on the eve of Waterloo,' to which General Airey replies, '*That was* a war'. Absurdity is added by the great statue of Wellington which sits outside Raglan's office, blocking his window, because no one knows what to do with it. At one point Raglan asks whether it could go on top of one of the new railway stations. This refers to a genuine incident of the time. Matthew Coates Wyatt, and his son James, modelled a colossal statue of the duke on horseback. It took three years to construct, weighed 40 tons, was 30 feet high and 26 feet long. When completed it took many months to plan its final home and unveiling. In 1846 it was placed on a triumphal arch at Hyde Park Corner with a great deal of ceremony and some satirical comments and cartoons in *Punch*. In 1882 the statue was taken down and moved to Aldershot because of new traffic arrangements for Hyde Park Corner.

By presenting Wellington in this way, it is hard not to wonder whether Richardson was not only lampooning Victorian society but the great imperial films of the 1930s and '40s as well. In Korda's *The Four Feathers* (1939), C. Aubrey Smith constantly recites the tales of his military career, including one about the Charge of the Light Brigade. His own memories and exploits are the standard by which all young men need to judge themselves. Richardson seems to be joking at the expense of the wise, old men of the imperial screen as well. But, to be fair, C. Aubrey Smith plays his role with a comic edge, emphasising the overblown tales of an old man. However, the theme of *The Four Feathers* is one which supports traditional codes of honour, chivalry and British moral supremacy.

Richardson therefore presents the army as a microcosm of British society. It is seen to be hide-bound, inefficient, nasty, brutish and petty-minded. Those who want to reform it are young, but they are not necessarily that much more rational. After all, Nolan, like Cardigan, lives for the thrill of the fight.

This world meets its Waterloo in the Crimea. Richardson presents the war with documentary reality, with an incredible eye for detail and as a bitterly ironic cartoon exaggeration. Such a combination is visually stunning and shocking, while the screenplay builds up to a sabre-sharp finale.

For Richardson, Britain was a nation easily whipped up into war fever. It is quite literally a war fever, for no one is too sure why Britain is fighting. Parallels with Vietnam arise here. We see an anti-war meeting and hear a clergyman announce to the crowd that there 'are hardly any issues involved'. This meeting is then violently broken up by Cardigan's troopers. They ride across the podium, slashing at the banners and scattering the crowd. Two images come to mind. First, the television news coverage of the treatment of anti-Vietnam War protesters in both America and Britain. Second, images from Eisenstein movies. The troopers rushing in to quell any element of free speech and peaceful protest are reminiscent of the bloodthirsty cavalrymen of *Strike* or *Battleship Potemkin*. Once again, it was a scene mirrored in *Oh! What a Lovely War* for it shows an anti-war meeting led by Mrs Pankhurst (aptly played by Vanessa Redgrave) broken up by mindless, patriotic rabble-rousers.

Raglan, being obsessed by his service with the duke, constantly confuses the French for the enemy rather than an ally. He tells Airey: 'I do think the French have been asking for it for some time.' No one is sure where the Crimea is, and Raglan asks Nolan for a map for he does not know where he is. Sebastopol is even more of a mystery. General Scarlett is told they are going for Sebastopol and he remarks, 'But I don't want any damned Sebastopols.' When explaining the cause of the war and British objectives to his generals, Raglan says: 'Our passage to India is threatened [pause] I should think, shouldn't you?' The overall impression is of the blind leading the blind in a black comedy. Even in the Crimea he is unsure what he is up to and who the enemy is. While resting at his billet he sees French cavalry enter the yard. Thrown into a panic he yells out to Airey that they are surrounded and the French are upon them. Airey reminds him that the French are their allies. Of course, the loss of an arm at Waterloo caused by a French cannon ball is one of those details that has to be true – if it were invented by a scriptwriter the audience would think the joke had been taken too far.

The arrival of the British Expeditionary Force off the Crimean coast is used to highlight the hideousness of the passage. A huge storm rocks the ship containing the hussars and their unfortunate horses. Richardson creates a scene of great power as torrents of water wash down the gangways and deluge the holds containing the stalls of the horses. The horses' cries add to the crash of the waves and the roar of the wind and the creak of timbers. Next we see the cadavers of the horses dumped into the now quiet waters. Rather shockingly, the awful bloated corpses float around the ship. It is not only shocking, it is actually rather surreal. Once again reality provides a neat twist, for Nolan turns to his friend and says: 'Tomorrow, Calamita Bay – is it aptly named do you think, William?'

The disembarkation at Calamita is a truly amazing piece of cinema, a vast panoply of action and colour. Barges move in-shore, crowded with scarlet-coated troops, bagpipes skirl, horses splash through the foam, white-uniformed, straw-boatered sailors help men ashore. Richardson's command of the situation is obvious in this scene, teasing out the best from Watkin's camera. The scene begins with the sea lapping over the lens of the camera as barges drift past. David Watkin and his technicians built a special glass tank for the camera in order to shoot this sequence. It is arresting and beautiful, it also encourages a sense of exposure and vulnerability. Richardson then uses a few high shots giving the viewer a panorama of the landing. But much of the landing is shot in medium focus or close-up and at, or just below, eye-level. It creates a palpable feeling of dynamism and an equally powerful sense of being there, of feeling men and gear lumber ashore. The wheels of the cannons and guns slice through the spray as the spokes revolve in slow arcs, soaked horses clumsily wade through the rollers. At times it approaches the 'virtual reality' effect of *Saving Private Ryan*. In the midst of all this purposeful, if slightly chaotic dynamism, Raglan and Airey are brought ashore. But their arrival is hardly that of Henry V striding ashore in full armour, instead they are carried on the backs of two sailors and planted down next to the Union flag. It all looks like a ridiculous seaside party game, as does setting the Great War on Brighton pier in *Oh! What a Lovely War*. Just as Raglan touches down he sees a Highlander who has taken off his bearskin hat. He urges him to replace it, saying, 'It is your only protection against the sun.' After the drama of the storm and the sheer panache and bravado of the landings, the viewer is brought crashing back to the absurdity of the situation.

Richardson's use of the 'switchback' is then employed again, for the troops begin to form up and march off. The sight of thousands of troops marching across the ridge whistling military tunes, banners flying, is very stirring. Again, the scene is handled brilliantly. A long-shot slowly pans across the ridge, showing the men striding purposefully. It cuts to a close-up of the men's faces; they appear quite calm, happy even. A medium-shot then shows cavalrymen darting to and fro across the columns of troops. Movement, glamour, dash. A quick cut to a close-up of the regimental colours follows, creating a beautiful effect as the screen fills with the billowing silky golds and reds of the flags.

Then it cuts to close-up, on the soundtrack a drum taps out a melancholy tattoo, flies buzz and an unhealthy sepia light streams across the picture. The men are slumping in their saddles, sick, with ghastly complexions. Cholera is sweeping the ranks. The glory of their departure and the beauty of their uniforms are reduced to vomiting men clasping their guts. Lord Lucan rides up and down the columns yelling insults, telling the men to get up and not lie about like girls. Black comedy here becomes vicious vituperation.

The French armies are never seen in the film. To all intents and purposes the British seem to be fighting the Russians alone. The French commander, Marshal St Arnaud, a very old and very frail man, is treated as a doddering old fool by Raglan because he has a slightly eccentric manner. However, when the commanders meet to discuss the crossing of the river Alma, St Arnaud announces that his army will attack the flank while the British will go for 'the front door ... knock, knock' (he makes a knocking notion with his hand and chuckles). Raglan turns to Airey and states: 'He's not well, you know.' But Raglan is too dense to see the point: St Arnaud has wangled a much easier job for his armies and is leaving the dirty work to the daft British.

Raglan announces his orders for the attack in his usual bizarre language. 'Form the infantry *nicely* for the assault. And give them a smile, Airey; they always go off happier for a friendly face.' Sir George Brown roars out 'view-halloos' to his troops as he attempts to whip them up for the attack. In response, Raglan asks him to be quiet, for the 'halloos' are confusing his horse into thinking the fox hounds will be unleashed any second. The attack on the heights of Alma is yet another brilliant cinematic set-piece. The scarlet-coated infantrymen wade through the river and begin their laborious scaling of the steep escarpments. Sir Colin Campbell, the recklessly brave commander of the Highland Brigade, bawls at his men to leave all the wounded behind and then charges off at their head. The scenes are reminiscent of Roger Fenton's original photographs of the attack and the engravings in the *Illustrated London News*. Richardson's office in South Audley Street was covered in reproductions of Fenton's work as he sought to immerse himself in the feel of the time. David Watkin helped achieve this effect by stripping down his mounts in order to use an old-fashioned Ross Xpress lens in its heavy brass fittings. Richardson helped Watkin in this by being sublimely unconcerned about any possible protest from Panavision whose lenses had been supplied with the Samuelson equipment.[12] Just as the British troops fight their way through the black powder clouds and Russian lines, the scene cuts back to Raglan and his senior officers. At this moment Marshal St Arnaud slumps dead. With comic solemnity all the commanders take off their hats as a mark of respect and Raglan reminds them: 'I told you he wasn't well.' Nolan is impatient at such fiddling and demands the cavalry be sent into action in order to pursue the fleeing Russians and capture Sebastopol there and then. Fearing a huge row between Lucan and Cardigan, Raglan refuses to give the order and instead uses the cavalry to accompany the guns forward to the next objective. His overriding concern is to keep the two men apart. The military success of the campaign is subordinated to the ridiculous.

After witnessing the sombre pomp with which St Arnaud's passing is met and the pathetic reasoning of Raglan, the scene cuts to the heights of Alma. The vision of cheering troops fades to that of the desolation of the battlefield itself. Men lie in agony, their lovely uniforms ripped and covered in blood. There is very little dignity and there are confusing signals about the nature of humanity. A British soldier tries to help a wounded Russian, but is then shot by another Russian who attempts to rob him. In response Nolan shoots the looting Russian. It is a degrading and appalling vision. Ironically, the scene also recalls the dictum of the Duke of Wellington when asked whether a victory was a great thing: 'The greatest tragedy in the world, madam, except a defeat.'

Active service does nothing to lessen the petty rigours of military life. The lampooning of the Victorian army reaches greater heights once the troops establish themselves in camp around Sebastopol. The clumsy bell tents are erected with much hard labour. No sooner is this task completed than Cardigan arrives and tells the men the tents are not straight and orders them struck and re-erected. The whole palaver begins again. Once they have been re-erected Lucan turns up and announces that they are too close together and so they are pulled down again and moved. Mrs Duberly tells William Howard Russell: 'This is the second time today, put that down and tell them that at home.'

We know the pantomime is about to reach its climax when we see the overweight Cardigan being dragged, pushed and pulled into his breeches. The immediate reason for the hurry is a Russian attack on a line of British forts. It occurs under the eyes of Raglan who does very little to influence the situation. Raglan, for once, is not entirely to blame. He is paralysed by the refusal of one of his commanders to obey his orders. Sir George Brown says he cannot move himself, or his men, until he has had breakfast. He continues to eat his boiled egg. Once again, it is a moment that must be true because it lacks the credibility of fiction. Back with Raglan the confusion and inaction continue. They all sit and watch as the Russians hitch up the British guns and start dragging them off. Nolan is infuriated and urges Raglan to use the cavalry to cut off the Russians. Raglan finally agrees to do so and Nolan insists on taking the order to Lucan and Cardigan. The scene is dramatic and impressive, as Nolan rides off with great vigour. It almost seems like a homage to the Western, as Nolan is seen galloping alone in a slow long-shot, the camera panning along the dusty, brown ridge.

Sitting at the bottom, and the bottom end, of a Y-shaped valley, neither Cardigan nor Lucan can see the Russians removing the British guns. All they can see is the other arm of the valley where the Russians are dug in on three sides and have hundreds of cannon. They therefore receive Nolan and his orders with some incomprehension. The hot-headed Nolan cannot understand their reaction, waves his hand vaguely above his head and yells: 'There is the enemy, there are your guns.'[13]

4. *The attention to period detail is revealed in this shot of Alan Dobie (Mogg) and Corin Redgrave (Featherstonehaugh).*

The looks on the faces of Cardigan and Lucan show us that the tragic die is cast. Cardigan is going to charge the wrong valley. For the first time it is possible to feel some sympathy for Cardigan, for he is certainly not going to leave his men alone, he is going to face every danger with them; it is his redeeming feature. As Cardigan and his men begin their slow trot, Nolan looks around him. He begins to understand the confusing nature of the geography. Suddenly, seized with panic, he starts to yell and wave his sword above his head, trying vainly to gain the attention of the Light Brigade. He wants to regroup them and lead them in the right direction. But the robot-like routine of the men cannot be altered. Indeed, Nolan's friend believes it is just a piece of vainglory on Nolan's part, trying to lead the charge instead of being a part of it, and he cries after him that such things aren't done.[14] At that moment Nolan's cries merge into the scream of a cannon shell which explodes, sending shrapnel ripping into his chest. He falls from his horse, blood and spittle pouring from his mouth. The charge is going down the wrong valley. Another shell explodes and the white smoke and red sparks merge into the white and red plumes on Raglan's hat. Richardson cuts back to the real fount of the confusion, the symbol of what David Jones called the 'monumental bollocks' of battle plans in his Great War epic, *In Parenthesis*.

However, this film is not a simple anti-war invective, for the charge is presented not as an entirely ironic or pointless episode. It is a thrilling sight and it is impossible not to admire the courage and skill of the men involved. Despite the incredible odds, they do reach the guns and do cause some damage to the Russians. Richardson's use of shots shows the same variety and confidence seen in earlier scenes. The close-ups of men's faces reveal the individual agony and fear of battle. Shots from waist-level emphasise the smallness and vulnerability of men in battle; again it is hard for a modern viewer not to compare it with *Saving Private Ryan*, for Richardson achieved the same feeling of being there, of being in the heat of battle. The long-shots, with the strange puffs of smoke and clouds of dust, imply the surreal, chaotic madness of battle. Richardson included close-ups of the recoils of the guns, cannon wheels shoot backwards, creating an awful sense of the dynamic, destructive power of modern weapons. It is only at this point that the atmosphere begins to change, that the viewer begins to ask, 'But where do they go now and what do they do?' Almost instantly the real irony hits the viewer. The Light Brigade has no alternative but to ride all the way back to its startline. The scene then cuts to the ridge from which Captain and Mrs Duberly, Russell and a few other civilians are picnicking and watching and waiting. A few riderless horses come out of the dust along with limping, wounded men. Captain Duberly reveals his utter ignorance by announcing the arrival of skirmishers. It is Russell who sees through this, correcting him that it is the Light Brigade.

The men stumble back in an terrible mess, sooty, bloody, some maimed and without limbs and utterly exhausted. They look very much like casualties of modern war; it is in fact a cinematic rendering of Wilfred Owen's lines from *Dulce et Decorum est*:

> Bent double, like old beggars under sacks,
> Knock-kneed, coughing like hags, we cursed through sludge,
> Till on the haunting flares we turned our backs,
> And towards our distant rest began to trudge.
> Men marched asleep. Many had lost their boots,
> But limped on, blood-shod. All went lame, all blind;
> Drunk with fatigue ...

Incredibly, though perhaps not entirely ironically, Cardigan's men cheer him when he arrives back and they ask him whether they are to go again, they will for him. He appears moved by this and replies: 'No, no, you have done enough today.' He further explains that the orders were nothing to do with him. But he cannot retain his dignity, for he immediately begins an attack on Nolan. He remarks, 'I will break him. How dare he to ride before the general of the brigade like that. Did you hear the creature shrieking like some tight girl, like a woman fetching off. Damn him. Damn all his kind. Nolan that Indian, miserable-arsed mutineer.' When he asks where Nolan is, he receives the sobering and curt reply: 'My lord, you have just ridden over his body.'[15]

Raglan arrives and an argument breaks out, for he asks Cardigan what on earth he has done. Calmly, Cardigan replies that he has carried out Lord Lucan's orders. This is enough for Raglan, he shifts the blame, saying that Lucan has lost the Light Brigade. Lucan, unsurprisingly, defends himself by reminding Raglan he was merely passing on his order and hands the paper to him. Raglan had dictated the order to Airey and the vague wording of the original is repeated verbatim in the movie. Raglan eyes it and announces: 'Not my handwriting ... Airey you have lost the Light Brigade.' Airey blurts out: 'I will not be blamed.' It is the signal for the gathered high command to start a squabble.[16] What a farce! As they argue the camera pulls back, we see horses being shot and then a bootless, blood-streaked Captain Morris wanders back, stumbling over the body of his dead friend, Nolan. Like Rupert Codrington, he was an innocent young soldier, now he is a man who has seen far too much. The sound of buzzing flies is heard. The camera settles on a dead horse and its dead rider. The scene freezes. The credits roll.

THE CHARGE OF THE LIGHT BRIGADE, WARNER BROTHERS, 1936

The great comparison with Richardson's version is, of course, the rightly famous 1936 film starring that ultimate hero of the costume film, Errol Flynn, and directed by Michael Curtiz.[17] It came at a time when Hollywood had a great interest in the British Empire and celebrated it as a world of romance, glamour and adventure in such films as *The Lives of a Bengal Lancer*, *Gunga Din* and *King Solomon's Mines*. Much of the film is set in India, following the adventures of British cavalrymen as they attempt to avenge the massacre of European and Indian women and children by an evil rebel emir. Only at the end of the movie does the scene switch to the Crimea, where the Lancers find out that the emir has fled India and has taken refuge with the Russians. The final, climactic charge therefore becomes an event of intense personal commitment to the men of the Light Brigade. They are there to mete out their own justice to a man who had ravaged their cantonment while they were on manoeuvres. Far from being a pointless waste of life, it is a quixotic, chivalrous action, anchored in the most honourable motives. For Warner Brothers the story was one of honour and chivalry, of men carrying out their tasks no matter what the personal risk because they believed in the highest of ideals, ideals that were enshrined in the British Empire: law, order, hierarchy, decency, dignity, courage. It is a very different understanding of the British Empire to that shown in the 1968 version. Richardson's aim was to unmask such values as mere hypocrisy and manipulative tricks. Though Richardson did not appear to have set out with the express idea of satirising the exciting, glorious romance of 1936, it is hard not to be aware of the yawning chasm dividing the films in terms of style, texture and understanding of the same historical event.

The difference in tone between the two films is best expressed in their respective treatments of love and army life. Olivia de Havilland, playing Elsa Campbell, daughter of Colonel Campbell (Donald Crisp), provides the love interest in Warner's version. Elsa is engaged to Geoffrey Vickers (Flynn), but while he has been away she has fallen in love with his brother Perry (Patric Knowles). We sympathise with Elsa's predicament; she clearly does not want to hurt Geoffrey but she has to be true to her heart. At first Geoffrey refuses to believe that she could love Perry; instead he believes Perry is trying to lure her away from him. This leads to a quarrel and an estrangement between the two brothers. Slowly, however, Geoffrey begins to realise that Elsa truly does love Perry. With honour and dignity Geoffrey withdraws from the scene and ensures that Perry will not accompany him in the final charge of the Light Brigade, thus giving the true lovers life at the expense of his own death. It is therefore a story of self-sacrifice, of dignity, of reconciliation and understanding.

Richardson's interpretation of the affair between Nolan and Clarissa is handled with a great deal of sensitivity, it is not mere sexual attraction that leads them to infidelity. It is a very different thing to the affairs of Lord Cardigan. But it is also subtly different to the 1936 version, for in Richardson's story there is a pregnancy in which paternity is unsure. It is also a genuine infidelity, not doubts before a marriage. Nolan's understanding of honour does not stop him from actually making love to a married woman. When she falls pregnant he leaves her without comfort, for him the child simply must be her husband's, it is nothing to do with him and he tears up her letter without reading it, throwing the pieces over the side of his troopship. In this sense war is not the resolution of the problem, as it is for Geoffrey, Perry and Elsa, but an escape from it.

Romantic drama in the Warner version is encapsulated in a ballroom scene. Ballroom scenes involving gloriously uniformed soldiers were a standard part of the 1930s costume drama. We see beautiful soldiers swirling around with gorgeous women in *Anna Karenina* (1935), for example, but the *Charge*'s closest imitator is Korda's *The Four Feathers* (1939). In both imperial movies the ballroom scene is a moment in which fiancées make troubling announcements to uniformed beaux. Elsa talks to Perry on the terrace as they discuss the best way to end her engagement to Geoffrey. In the *Four Feathers*, Ethne (June Duprez) has to tell Durrance (Ralph Richardson) that she is actually going to marry Feversham (John Clements).

Richardson could not resist the ballroom, for much the same reason as the earlier film-makers; great uniforms and beautiful women look even better when swirling round a fabulous set to the alluring strains of waltzes. However, for Richardson the ballroom scene is the moment in which old men talk utter twaddle or make crude sexual innuendos and the foundations for a traumatic infidelity are laid.

But it is in the presentation of army life, with its ranks and codes, that the earlier version shows the greatest variation from Richardson's work, revealing how cynical (as well as idealistic) the world had become by 1968. The two films make similar points about army life, but they come to entirely different conclusions. The army of the 1936 film is also one of class, rank and inheritance but it is not presented as a problem.

General Macefield (Henry Stephenson) tells Geoffrey: 'The Vickers are an old army family. I knew your father at Sandhurst.' An inheritance of service and dedication is presented as an asset to the nation, not a crippling, constricting vice. Geoffrey is impatient to get revenge on the evil emir, but he is told of the importance of obeying orders. He is reminded of the ancient family from which he has sprung and its long service tradition. 'When you've been a soldier for as long as I have,' says Colonel Campbell, 'you will learn that it is unwise to question orders.' Here is the moral of Tennyson's poem. The poem prefaces the film and stanzas appear on screen during the charge itself. But there is no real sense of someone having blundered in the movie. The troopers do not need to reason why, for they know why they are charging. They are fighting 'to prove to the world that no man can kill women and children and then boast of it'.

Britons are capable of incredible feats of heroism and self-sacrifice in this movie because they are brought up within a value system that has proved itself over time and has proved itself beneficent. Before this system is tested by the charge, we are presented with notable individual examples of accepting personal danger in order to help others. Vickers saves the life of the emir at the start of the film, even though he has doubts about his integrity. Later Captain Randall (David Niven) sacrifices his own life trying to raise the alarm on behalf of his besieged comrades. Officers therefore set an example, which the men are more than content to follow. Unlike Richardson's interpretation, these codes of honour have a genuine core and a genuine worth. Occasionally, officers are seen to make mistakes, but these are passed off as minor eccentric or comic traits rather than with the bitter irony of Richardson. General Benjamin Warrenton (Nigel Bruce) is presented as a hen-pecked, silly ass. He enjoys a secret tipple and rather blunders and bumbles around. But when the hideously dangerous task of charging the Russian guns is put to him, he accepts the order willingly for he knows it will bring the malevolent emir to book. He is a man with an innate sense of justice and right, a sense that overrides any other vices he might have.

In this film the charge is a willingly accepted suicide mission. Vickers, desperate to avenge the massacre in Chukoti, deliberately changes the orders of Macefield and deliberately ignores the good advice of Cardigan to withdraw the cavalry. Geoffrey also sends his brother off the battlefield with a despatch, thus saving him from certain death and freeing him to marry Elsa. He writes an explanation to Macefield, knowing the general will be blamed for the charge. However, Macefield, being a man of honour himself, burns the letter and faces the blame rather than allow anyone to question the actions of Vickers. It is yet another quixotic gesture in a movie full of them. The film fulfils its opening statement in which we see the Latin motto of the (fictional) 27th Lancers inscribed in stone: 'Who Shall Excel Them?'

It is too simplistic to say that the two films are completely different, have no common reference points or are poles apart. Rather, the point is that the two films have the same totem pole but the way they interpret the runes, symbols and images on the pole are completely different.

THREE
The Reception and the Years that Followed

The Charge of the Light Brigade had attracted press interest due to its long and expensive production. Having had their appetites whetted, film critics were keen to see the latest and most ambitious production yet of one of Britain's foremost young directors. However, controversy was about to descend, for Richardson took the decision, backed by Woodfall and United Artists, to scrap a press showing. If the press wanted to see it they could pay their money and go with the viewing public. Richardson penned a letter to *The Times* explaining his reasons. All forms of art criticism in Britain had become too biased, too obsessed with personal, petty debates, too interested in using influence to attack rather than constructively criticise, too in love with the power to break a production, he wrote. In a colourful phrase he referred to critics as 'a group of acidulated, intellectual eunuchs hugging their prejudices like feather boas'. He concluded: 'The important thing, above all, for a critic is to present the film to the public, not to get in between. Of course, alas, to get in between is just what our present critics want. It is best that the sorry lot stay away.'[1]

Such an assault was bound to have two effects. First, it raised the ire of much of Fleet Street. Second, it ensured the film was notorious before anyone saw a frame of it. A stampede of journalists began, all jostling to attack Richardson's attitude. The *Sun* trumpeted:

> If the critics were as hysterical and prejudiced in their attitude to films as Mr Richardson is in his attitude to the critics he really would have cause to complain. No doubt Mr Richardson would like the critics to say that every film — and particularly every film he makes — is wonderful. They would be a pretty easily pleased lot if they did.[2]

The *New Statesman* claimed Richardson's letter made 'sad reading', and added that he was sulking at not getting the praise he thought he deserved.[3] A similar air of bitchiness pervaded the *Guardian*, where Philip Hope-Wallace sniped at 'the over-praised Mr Richardson'.[4]

Felix Barker, of the film section of the Critics' Circle, issued a statement on the matter. Many newspapers published extracts from it, including the *Evening News* under the headline, 'Ban on Critics for Royal Film Show'. Barker hinted at a complete boycott of the movie: 'While wholeheartedly condemning this restricted attitude which denies all fundamental principles of free speech, we have decided that each editor must act in the way he thinks best and decide the best means with which he wishes to deal with this film.' He went on to deny that 'we ever wish "to get in between" a film and its public appreciation ... Most critics are deeply concerned with their responsibility to the creative artist whose thought and craftsmanship go into a film.'[5]

Richardson had ruffled the feather boas, revealing an incredible sensitivity among critics, a sensitivity they rarely use when examining other people's work. Fascinatingly, they took the line that the ban was a restriction of free speech. This seems subtly to misconstrue the nature of Richardson's argument. He was not denying the critics their right to see the film, but he was not going to let them see it for nothing, with corporate hospitality provided. *The Charge of the Light Brigade* had been a matter of press speculation throughout its production, it was now awaited with an obsessive fascination.

Having viewed the film the critics were remarkably measured and careful in their responses. This may have been a riposte to Richardson, showing that critics do not heap hyperbolic praise or dissent as the whim takes them. A few even liked it, but in a hesitant, qualified way. Many critics praised the rich, beautiful look of the film. Alexander Walker picked up on this in the *Evening Standard*, and the *Daily Express* remarked on its 'beautiful production'. Patrick Gibbs, writing in the *Sunday Telegraph*, referred to it as 'ravishing' and noted how carefully each shot had been prepared by Richardson and David Watkin. He also praised the sense of period style; he felt a strong air of Burne-Jones and Millais, rightly noting that the film was at its strongest whenever Vanessa Redgrave was in view. *The Sun* noted that, though 'a disappointment in some ways, [it] is still an epic of quality, both in performance and presentation'.[6]

Those who liked it also joined those critics who found it too muddled and confusing. Many felt that Richardson had not made up his mind about what kind of film he wanted to make. Was it meant to be a huge, adventure epic or a bitterly ironic comment? Unfortunately, few asked whether it was meant to be both. Ian Wright of the *Guardian* was confused, was it 'ironic, epic, naturalistic'?[7] For the *Daily Express* an opportunity to create a truly great film had been missed: 'If its aim had been clearer, its attitude more consistent, if it had rambled less and concentrated more, it could have been a great one.'[8] Patrick Gibbs compared the film with Woodham-Smith's original text, noting the clarity of her work and the disorganisation of Richardson and Wood's. The British obsession with being faithful to the facts at all times, of creating films out of facts – the phenomenon that led to the Crown Film Unit drama-documentaries of the Second World War receiving so much praise – was in evidence again. But Margaret Hinxman, also writing in the *Sunday Telegraph*, combated such views. For her, the story demanded a sense of caricature, for it was a genuinely grotesque and baroque tale: 'To say that this is a slanted picture of Victorian life, that the period also spawned men of vision, conscience and genius, is to miss the point. If you're going to make an accurate film about the Crimean War this is the film it probably has to be.'[9]

Running alongside the criticisms of its muddled nature were criticisms of the battle scenes themselves. For Gibbs the camera failed to make clear the nature of the terrain and so it did not explain how or why the Light Brigade charged the wrong valley. Alexander Walker noted that the charge was 'over and done with almost before it's begun'.[10] (By way of contrast Kevin Brownlow had written in his notes, 'the direction of the action is inspired'.)[11]

One element, at least, did come in for unqualified praise and that was the animation. Richard Williams had plaudits piled on him stretching from *Playboy* to the *Financial Times*. *Playboy* noted the vital element of continuity his animations provided for the film, while the *Financial Times* felt the influence of the original *Punch* and *Illustrated London News* cartoons and called him 'one of the finest animation artists in the world'. Pauline Kael believed the animations were the only saving grace of the film: 'The rulers and military leaders actually blend into interpolated animation (by Richard Williams) that is remarkably witty and effective in itself. The animation provides the only clear exposition we get of what's going on in the movie. It's too bad Richardson didn't leave the Charge itself to Williams.' In complete contrast, Donald Zec, cartoonist of the *Daily Mirror*, saw the animated opening sequence as the herald of a triumphant movie: 'When an audience applauds the titles of a film, you can sense something out of the ordinary is to follow.'[12]

Nothing could make Ernest Betts of the *Sunday People* write a good

5. *David Hemmings as Captain Nolan. Charles Wood's play* Veterans, *based on the making of* The Charge of the Light Brigade, *made many arch comments on the horsemanship of a thinly disguised David Hemmings.*

review of the film. Much of his review is filled with the spirit of his initial complaint: having to pay to get in! He sourly concluded: 'I don't share the view of some of my colleagues that this film, which is violently anti-war, is a masterpiece.'[13] The implication seems to be that anti-war films can never be masterpieces. One wonders what he thought of *All Quiet on the Western Front.*

The specialist and trade press were also mixed in their response. *Kine Weekly* felt it was a quality film with great money-making potential,[14] but the *Monthly Film Bulletin* found very little to enjoy, indeed, it launched a step-by-step dissection of the film. The language and style of the review is so bitter as to make it a most entertaining read. It started with the premise that: 'Richardson was right in attempting to keep it away from the critics. Subjected to any kind of critical analysis, the film becomes a well-nigh intolerable mess, meandering, fidgety and indeterminate, trying with frequent signs of panic to reduce its subject nearer to manageable size by scurrilously simplifying and belittling the characters and events of the Crimean War.' This was just the warm-up for the real assault, for Richardson's skill as a director was subjected to detailed condemnation: 'Whether flogging Norman Rossington, dumping subjective comments on the soundtrack at uncertain intervals, pouring tons of water over a small group of horses and extras to simulate a storm at sea, or pinching a touch of lewdness from *Tom Jones*, Richardson has become little more than an amorphous catalytic agent in a mêlée of wildly disparate elements.' Continuing the line of vituperation, it attacked the 'monumental chaos' of the 'bungled film' and turned its attention to Charles Wood's script. Here the problem, according to the reviewer, was the lack of a script. It was felt that the actors were left to make it up as they went along. Gielgud and Howard were praised for improvising with panache and style, but Hemmings was blamed for getting 'himself lost right from his first scene', and Redgrave smiles 'vacuously', having detected 'that her presence is irrelevant'. The final damning line condemns the film for being 'magnificent, but it isn't cinema'.[15] This was a deliberate variation on General Bosquet's comment on the charge, '*c'est magnifique, mais ce n'est pas la guerre*'. Wood probably got to the real motivation behind these comments when he told me: 'There was something about our tone, our attitude, our confidence, that jarred with the audiences ... We were considered "too clever by half".'[16]

Richardson undoubtedly got off lightly from the mainstream press by comparison with the mood of the trade journals. And the sub-text of the trade journals does appear to be resentment at the 'too clever by half' approach of Richardson and his team.

The film's critical reception in the USA was much the same as in Britain, a mixture of qualified praise and some bafflement. The *New York Times* enjoyed the look, the performances and animation sequences. However, it did not feel that there was any modern relevance and clearly did not pick up on the latent criticism of Vietnam. There was a feeling that the film was too confused and confusing for its own good:

> Tony Richardson's *The Charge of the Light Brigade* comes very close to suffering the fate of the mule who, caught equidistant between two bales of hay, starved to death.
>
> But about half-way through, the movie that hasn't been able to make up its mind whether to be a political cartoon or a social history opts for the single dimensional approach. The result ... is a scathing, cryptic, sometimes brilliantly detailed caricature, which I'm sure is quite accurate as far as it goes but ... it has lost a bit of relevance.[17]

Interestingly, the critic felt the film could only suffer by comparison with the earlier version. But any viewer taking his or her expectations and knowledge of the charge from Curtiz's film and the Tennyson poem was bound to be baffled by Richardson's approach. Ultimately, the film was judged as 'high, entertaining dudgeon, but it's approximately 114 years too late'.

Variety was generally more enthusiastic. Cast, cinematography, the script and the animation were all highly praised, and its report was headlined: 'Well produced epic with satirical qualities. Title, theme and fine acting will excite wicket activity.' In opposition to the *New York Times*, it felt that the 1936 version could only help Richardson's, saying it was 'a magnet for customers by itself'. It was also an appraisal much more in tune with the film's anti-war stance, referring to the 'bitter irony', the 'grave imbecility of war' and, most powerfully, 'as a protest against war ... [it] is worth a flock of the World War II pix that have tried to put over their anti-war messages'. However, it was also noted that American audiences would take time to adapt to the English accents and historical idiom. Further, those who came expecting 'pure' epic might be disappointed. But generally it was a much more confident and up-beat appraisal than any other assessment.[18]

So how well did the film fare at the box-office? Were people prepared to pay to see it? The film was released in Britain on 10 April to a Royal Première, its US release followed a few days later. Following the established custom, the film was not shown anywhere else, in the capital or in the provinces, until it had completed a decent run at a single, major West End cinema (in this case the Odeon Leicester Square). After one week *Kine Weekly* declared it a 'smash', for it had taken an exceptionally good £20, 962.[19] A few weeks later it reported that the film had 'hardly felt the effect of the seasonal drift ... confirm[ing] its staying power', having taken £13,264 that week.[20] At the end of June, it was transferred to the Metropole, Victoria. United Artists took out a full-page advertisement in *Kine Weekly* confirming that the *Charge* had made £130,000 so far.[21] By the end of August, when it completed its West End first run, it had taken a further £35,000.[22] Unfortunately, *Kine Weekly* provides no figures as to its performance in the provinces, though Rank reported good figures for its south-east circuit.[23] It is therefore very hard to ascertain a final profit figure for the film. In December, when *Kine Weekly* completed its round-up of the year's big profit-makers, it appeared in the top ten, behind the year's best performers, *Doctor Zhivago* and *The Sound of Music*. But, once again, the journal fails to provide figures, showing only that the *Charge* was also accompanied by films such as *2001: A Space Odyssey*, *Far from the Madding Crowd*, *The Graduate*, *A Man for All Seasons* and *Thoroughly Modern Millie*.

In the USA the takings were poor, despite *Variety*'s instincts. Within a few weeks *Variety* was reporting that 'it looks to be in trouble' in New York and described subsequent weeks' receipts as 'modest', 'light', 'mild' and 'slow'. On the West Coast it was even worse, with takings less than a quarter of those in New York. In Los Angeles business was described as 'tame', 'slender', 'slim', 'dull' and 'dim'. A major problem of the film was clearly its perceived Britishness, the lack of advertising surrounding it, and it does not appear to have been screened in many places outside the large coastal cities.[24] Exactly the same problem was experienced by the equally expensive *Far from the Madding Crowd*.

Having cost so much to make, having been so long in the making and having had such high expectations, Woodfall, Richardson and United Artists can only have been very disappointed at its performance. Some of the problems the movie faced in America were probably applicable to Britain. Despite the interest in Victoriana, a tale about an obscure war in which a mad action took place was not, on first glance, a particularly appealing prospect. Further, it was a film that suffered from appearing not to know its own mind – too many people were unprepared to see it as both epic and satire; they wanted it to be one or the other. 'It was like calling something *Ben Hur* and then not doing the chariot race,' Kevin Brownlow replied when asked about its box-office failure. He continued: 'Everybody was waiting for the moment, the supreme action sequence which would dominate the picture, which would be glorious. What they did not want was a film which made them depressed, told the truth about war, which showed men dying of cholera.'[25]

One suspects that word of mouth had much to do with its lack of continued success. It also suffered when compared with its namesake, the very well loved and fondly remembered Flynn vehicle. Richardson seems to have guessed as much, for he noted in his autobiography that he should have titled it *The Reason Why* instead.[26] In fact *The Reason Why* seems a far more appropriate title for the movie. It would have silenced the critics who claimed to have been baffled by the battle scenes, for the point of the film is that the Light Brigade was doomed long before Nolan vaguely swung his hand above his head.

However, in examining its box-office performance it has to be noted that it did very well during its West End release. It was a great pity it was forced to move from the Odeon, due to that cinema's other booking commitments, as it had built up a 'good head of steam' there. For many, however, the film confirmed doubts about Richardson's work, and it was to take a long time for the *Charge* to reclaim its place as a major British movie and perhaps the last great British epic.

THE REPUTATION OF *THE CHARGE OF THE LIGHT BRIGADE* SINCE 1968

The true worth of *The Charge* has been a point of contention ever since its original release. Debate has centred on a few major points. Much confusion has been expressed over whether the movie was deliberately designed to meet the criteria of an epic. This is understandable, for the film is certainly epic in scale and scope, filling every inch of the screen from first to last, and yet it also seems to snipe at many of the conventions of the heroic epic. Alexander Walker felt potential audiences were kept away by this fact.[27] George Lellis, writing in *Sight and Sound* in 1969, also found the film ambiguous in this respect. He commented: 'Sea-storms, cholera attacks, cavalry charges, and floggings (an ominous inclusion for the first part of the picture) are the standard conventions of the epic.'[28] He implied this was almost a 'paint by numbers' approach, which ill fitted the other aims of the film.

Springing from this confusion, and very similar to it, was the problem of the name of the movie and its relationship with the 1936 film. 'I expected everyone to realise what this film was designed to do ... I thought we'd get away with it,' Kevin Brownlow said on considering the comparison with the earlier film.[29] Charles Wood noted: 'I think that people were expecting Errol Flynn again but this need not have mattered. Most people simply wanted "the charge" part of the film to go on longer.'[30] The desire of audiences to relive the thrills of the 1936 version has continued to dog the film. This is a little surprising, for any intelligent viewer can see it is not meant to be a remake, a homage, or even a direct critique of Curtiz's film. David Watkin claimed it never even entered his head to think about the Flynn film.[31] Even so, Robert and Gwendolyn Nowlan, in their work *Cinema Sequels and Remakes, 1903-1987*, still felt cheated that the film was not more in tune with Flynn and chums and persisted in seeing Richardson's work as a remake and direct, rather than oblique, comparator: 'The remake contained some splendid moments but on the whole was rather disappointing. No one in the cast, certainly not David Hemmings, had the charisma of Flynn. The whole thing seemed to lack direction as if the producers and director were trying to tell several stories, rather than one rousing adventure yarn.'[32] Unwittingly, the Nowlans identify one of the themes of the film: it is telling several stories rather than concentrating on one rousing adventure yarn.

In a very interesting and perceptive piece written for the *Film Society Review*, John Craddock argued that if Richardson's work was to be compared to the 1936 version then it must be seen in terms of direct contrast rather than compatibility. 'Richardson may have wished to correct the record left by the earlier Warner Brothers film.'[33]

Richardson's crucial satirical thread has also caused much controversy. In adopting an ironic position the film took a highly stylised line. This stylisation then left it open to the criticism of being inaccurate. But, of course, any such judgement depends on how one defines accuracy. By exaggeration and stylisation, Richardson and Wood seem to get at the spirit of the age, even if it occasionally loses absolute documentary authenticity. For Kevin Brownlow 'the spirit is accurate', and he believes only David Lean's *Oliver Twist* and *Great Expectations* have got as close to the atmosphere of nineteenth-century Britain.[34] However, for some this has proved a major problem. George MacDonald Fraser, author of the highly popular 'Flashman' novels concerning the adventures of the bully of *Tom Brown's School Days*, clearly has no time for Richardson's work. In his study of history on film, *The Hollywood History of the World*, he condemned almost every aspect of the movie, bemoaning the fact that 'Lord Raglan, the army commander, was an ass, but not the kind of ass John Gielgud makes him. I don't know on what authority Mrs Duberly can be accused of misconduct, but if none exists (and I have heard of none) then her portrayal in the film is inexcusable.'[35]

Others have realised that such liberties led to a powerful study of the nature of Victorian Britain. Alexander Walker felt the film worked as 'a savagely illuminating period reconstruction with an excoriating running commentary on the class system and military castes'.[36] George Lellis felt a similar sense of accuracy, derived through a highly stylised and satirical filter: 'On the whole ... in his grotesque portrayal of nineteenth century military stupidity, Richardson attains, with the help of Charles Wood's very good Victorian dialogue, a view that is funny, dry, and detachedly observant.'[37] Fascinatingly, Charles Wood has defended the film on the sort of grounds MacDonald Fraser would probably appreciate. He has claimed its critics have never got into the real spirit of the thing, for they 'haven't got pissed Balaclava day or sent telegrams to the others – the other remnants of famous regiments now defunct or the Umpty-Umptieth-Umpty Queens something – congratulating them'.[38] The real problem with judging the authenticity of Richardson's work is very definitely one of perspective. For those, like MacDonald Fraser, who appear to believe cinema should never attack British institutions, Richardson's work is certainly anathema. However, he and his like appear to accept uncritically the use of history to create melodrama and romance. But if one is prepared to accept Errol Flynn and Basil Rathbone as Robin Hood and the Sheriff of Nottingham in Curtiz's excellent, but one suspects totally inaccurate, *The Adventures of Robin Hood* (1938), then one should also accept Richardson's interpretation of the past. Craddock pointed out that 'any serious historical film labors under a heavy handicap. In a field that has been dominated almost entirely by the distortions of sword opera, audiences have come to demand adventure above accuracy. Even when the historical detail is accurate, it is a mere backdrop to romance.'[39] Critics of Richardson's style of understanding do not appear to be consistent when dealing with the historical romance because it affirms rather than attacks or satirises.

Because Richardson attempted the very tricky task of using epic scale while maintaining a satirical edge, the farcical element has also inspired confusion and condemnation. MacDonald Fraser had no time for the stress on fiasco above heroism:

> By concentrating a good deal on preliminaries to the campaign and to the charge itself, with no great clarity, the film really does not help the seeker after truth; it seems more intent on correcting the popular view of Balaclava as a glorious catastrophe, and taking an altogether sourer view. God knows there is enough about the Crimea to make anyone sour, but not, I would suggest, the Charge of the Light Brigade. One leaves the film feeling that the six hundred deserved better.[40]

It is impossible to argue that this judgement is completely wrong, but the argument loses validity by being equally convinced that alternative interpretations of the charge are irrelevant or vicious. One might also say that for as long as events such as the Charge of the Light Brigade are regarded as glorious catastrophes, rather than as an appalling and incompetent waste of brave, skilled and loyal men, we are doomed to repeat them. Richardson and Wood never belittled the ordinary troopers, soldiers and junior officers – they also had a 'boys' own' relish in showing their bravery and skill – but they never spared the foolish men at the top who led them.

Richard Eyre has picked up on Wood's understanding of the ordinary soldier and interprets it as part of an overall indictment of the soldier's trade, without insulting the men called upon to carry out appalling tasks:

> Charles' seam is not so much warfare as the profession of soldiering, and the point of being a soldier is to break the ultimate taboo – the point is to destroy the enemy on our behalf, to kill people. This apparently self-evident truth is hidden from the recruit by the seductive panoply of uniforms, gold braid, pipes, drums, marching, medals, and the promise of adventure. Charles writes lovingly of all this but his invariable conclusion is that, for all the chivalry and courage, no war, just or unjust, can be acquitted of bestiality: the means never justify the ends. His indictment of war is invoked like a litany: it isn't worth it, it isn't worth it, it isn't worth it.[41]

Clearly, Richardson's and Wood's work provokes strong opinions and many different interpretations. As with every other aspect of the movie's reputation, the question of its true intentions has been fiercely debated. Many critics and commentators have been baffled by its ambiguity. Was the ambiguity a deliberately created effect, an elaborate conceit or evidence that Richardson lost control of the production and over-reached his skills as a director? The overall judgement is that Richardson did not keep a tight enough rein (if that is the appropriate image) on the production. Andy Medhurst has referred to the film's sprawling and confusing nature, raising issues it fails to follow through, with the whole thing all 'too often coming across as lack of focus'. Ironically, however, he compares it unfavourably with *Oh! What a Lovely War*, for if any film has been condemned as sprawling, unfocused and drifting it is Richard Attenborough's directorial debut.[42] Jeffrey Richards has referred to it as being 'highly enjoyable', but at the same time 'a pudding with all the ingredients thrown in'.[43] For George Lellis,

6. *'Watch the pretty valley.' Lord Raglan (John Gielgud) gives Mrs
Duberly (Jill Bennett) some typically eccentric advice on military
matters as the Light Brigade begins its fateful advance.*

too, Richardson created a pudding of many tastes. Using somewhat
arch language he noted that:

> As art it contains, back to back, the very best and very worst of this
> aesthetically ambiguous director, for the best becomes in turn, that which
> makes the worst worth talking about ... It is unfortunate to have to say
> that Richardson's cinematic hits are both overrated and over-evaluated
> and that his flops are in kind, underrated and under-evaluated.[44]

Lellis then implied that Eisenstein would have produced a much better
film out of the basic elements of the story.[45] Even John Craddock, a
fierce defender of the film, conceded that 'story continuity is not always
Richardson's strongest point', but he felt the film was deliberately ambiguous and vague, adding to the questioning and probing atmosphere
of the whole.[46]

Unlike many other critics, however, Craddock believed the film 'falls
little short of being a masterpiece'.[47] Perhaps unsurprisingly, Vanessa
Redgrave has taken a similar view. She wrote in her autobiography: 'I

thought it one of the best films about the British Empire and war ever made'; and in a letter to the author she wrote: 'Of course I think it is a masterpiece of any cinema and certainly a British cinema mountain peak.'[48] Trevor Howard told his biographer: 'I was disappointed that *The Charge of the Light Brigade* was not better received. It was not without its faults but I always felt that it had some marvellous moments.'[49]

There are two truly marvellous things about the *Charge*. First, it is an epic, a British epic. It more than fills the screen for the two and a bit hours of its running time. As Andy Medhurst has pointed out, this alone made it a great British film, especially when compared to the small-scale affairs British cinema churned out in the 1980s and 1990s.[50] Most modern British movies look as if they have been cut from cloth specially suited to look good on television. Richardson's effort was genuinely heroic by contrast, and if it is a failure, it is at least a heroic one. Second, it has a real sense of commitment, even if it does seem confused at times. For some this overt commitment has made it an unsubtle instrument. Jeffrey Richards referred to its ability to come down on the viewer with 'all the finesse of a steam hammer'.[51] The message comes straight out of the screen, punching the viewer. Its cry of protest and rebellion is very obvious.

Perhaps it is unfair to single out the *Charge* for its lack of subtlety, for it is a complaint that could be made about the entire decade. Richardson's film was a child of its time, showing all the traits of its time. It was also, very definitely, an allegory of its time. Few commentators realised this on its release, but it has been noted since.

War is shown to be a hellish, confusing experience; it is therefore impossible not to think of Vietnam when looking at the self-confident, bumbling British, unable to come to terms with the local conditions. Craddock believed Richardson and Wood were drawing parallels between the Anglo-French foray in the Suez Crisis, as well as pointing towards Vietnam.[52] Wood, however, is still sceptical of the Vietnam comparison. Instead, he sees it as a 'warning against the sort of adventures that we are undertaking now in places like Kosova'.[53] As a country that had been transformed by the Suez incident and the continuing retreat from empire, Britain had a very different social atmosphere according to Craddock. He argued it was now possible to make such questioning films in Britain, whereas US society had not yet learned the lesson that superpower status does not necessarily guarantee victory nor a monopoly on wisdom and morality. At the time of the *Charge*'s failure at the box-office, American audiences were flocking to see *The Green Berets* and *The Dirty Dozen*. Both films emulated and built upon the Second World War combat movie genre, ultimately sending reassuring messages of American righteousness and American victory.[54] For Craddock the parallel was potent and obvious: 'There is much in 19th-Century Britain and its problems that resembles the crises facing Americans today. The recruits who volunteered for the Crimean War fought not for love of country but for an essentially alien aristocracy, much as many black Americans feel that they are fighting for "whitey" in Viet Nam today.'[55]

George Lellis, too, remarked upon the fact that 'the resultant contemporaneity of the tale is certainly rewarding'.[56] The movie was therefore 'very much a film for and of our time'.[57]

In recent years Richardson's movie has undergone something of a renaissance, revealing a change of atmosphere and understanding. As mentioned earlier, the sense of scale and commitment is an important part of the film and has certainly helped revive its fortunes. Many British movies today seem either bloodless and/or made for a small eye looking at a small screen. Richardson died in late 1991 and *The Charge of the Light Brigade* was given screenings at NFT1 on 17 and 18 May 1992. Accompanying the screening, *Sight and Sound* carried articles by Charles Wood, Vanessa Redgrave and Andy Medhurst commenting on the film (all of which have been quoted in this work). Connoisseur Video then released a new copy of the film in widescreen format. At last it appears that the film can be discussed properly, with its strengths and weaknesses contextualised in an atmosphere significantly different to the sniping and bitterness that existed between the film-maker and the critics in the late 1960s.

CHARLES WOOD'S *VETERANS*

Having caused such a stir, and having been such an extraordinary project from start to finish, it is not surprising that *The Charge of the Light Brigade* inspired an alternative legend of its production. In his play, *Veterans*, Charles Wood confirmed with comic brilliance many of the stereotypical visions of the great British actors who appeared in the film.

Veterans provides a fascinating slant on the making of *The Charge of the Light Brigade*. The play concerns the shooting of a film about the Indian Mutiny being made in Turkey. The leading figures are Sir Geoffrey Kendle and Laurence D'Orsay, known to all as Dotty. Kendle is clearly meant to be Sir John Gielgud, while D'Orsay is Trevor Howard. There is also a Bryan David, who bears a resemblance to David Hemmings, and Trevor Hollingshead, who seems to be Tony Richardson.

Wood portrayed D'Orsay as a rather pathetic character. Known for his strong, macho film roles, D'Orsay is really quite unsure of himself and lacking in confidence. His friend, Kendle, knows this and tries to explain his character to other people. Kendle's dialogue provides strong hints that D'Orsay is Trevor Howard:

> oh I know he did all those
> stiff upper lip things and station platform
> things with the girls early on,
> tremendously successful, and *Target for*
> *Tonight* was a feather in his cap,
> everybody notices him in it, *F for Freddie*,
> one of our aircraft is missing,
> D for Dotty ... was he in *Target for Tonight*?[58]

In a characteristic muddle, Kendle gets it half right, half wrong. The station platform reference is clearly *Brief Encounter*, but he confuses *Target for Tonight* and *One of Our Aircraft is Missing* with another RAF drama, *The Way to the Stars*, in which Howard played a taciturn squadron leader. Wood deliberately stopped short of directly identifying Howard, but the references are clear enough. D'Orsay is accused of being difficult to get along with and prone to drink despite, or probably because of, his lack of inner confidence. Howard's biographer, Michael Munn, confirmed this trait and noted that Howard felt greatly honoured to work alongside Gielgud in *The Charge of the Light Brigade*, desperately wanting to match his performance.[59]

The character of Sir Geoffrey Kendle revealed Wood's skill at beguiling and intriguing his audience, especially an audience aware of Gielgud's portrayal of Raglan. Wood's dialogue for Kendle makes it seem as if Gielgud and Raglan were in fact one and the same person, for Kendle's character is as eccentric and bemusing as Wood's interpretation of Raglan. *Veterans* leads one to wonder whether Wood allowed Gielgud to play himself as Raglan and then noted down the great actor's character and style for later use. Raglan/Kendle/Gielgud appear to share the same eccentric understanding of the world. When Kendle makes a comment about the Turks, it reveals the Raglan traits of bizarre insights and slightly odd syntax:

I thought the Turks liked the sun in their
eyes for religious reasons,
seems a fallacy,
like us not eating fish on Fridays, I
do invariably[60]

Bryan David, on the other hand, is young, vigorous, anxious to confirm his reputation as an actor and ever so slightly pompous. Despite his image as a stud, he seems to be worried about his own sexuality. David Hemmings certainly had that sort of aura about him. Young, ambitious, glamorous and yet perhaps a bit too suave to be straight. Further, just as Kendle has a connection with the character of Raglan, David touches upon that of Nolan.

The behind-the-scenes story of *The Charge of the Light Brigade* is revealed most forcefully in Kendle's loathing and fear of his horse. Wood re-created Gielgud's well-known disdain for his mount for comic effect:

I shall never get
used to horses, all my years.

The nimble gunner!
Oh. Oh dear me the nimble gunner.

Poor fellows, they do well to be nimble,
I was myself near dragged like Hector
through shameful field,
through no fault of my own in beastly sort,
I would have been, my sword knot caught
in the wheels of a moving gun[61]

Whenever possible, Kendle sits on a box, rather than mount a real horse. But this leads to friction with David, whose macho image demands that he show off his horse-riding skills. *The Charge of the Light Brigade* shows Hemmings's riding technique to good effect, particularly in the scene in which he delivers Raglan's fateful message.

Kendle's other obsession is his great sword knot. He is convinced it will catch on something and cause an accident or ruin a scene. But he also knows there is a desire to be as accurate as possible and so frets about it. D'Orsay tells Kendle to cut it off, which just makes him all the more flustered. Once again it becomes hard to know the difference between Raglan, Kendle and Gielgud:

It is surprising
what does notice, you know that, and those
poor fellows hacking away at each other
get into dreadful trouble if they don't
dress properly. No, I think I ought to try
to manage with it, I'll ask if I can
be kept away from guns ... they were
awfully kind about it and made a great
deal of fuss, far too much fuss[62]

Veterans was first performed at the Royal Court Theatre on 9 March 1972. D'Orsay was played by John Mills, and Bryan David by Frank Grimes. But the whole thing must have been a near surreal experience, for Sir John Gielgud took the role of Sir Geoffrey Kendle. It must have been impossible to guess where reality and art began and ended.

Charles Wood retained a fascination with army life and the strange impulse to make war. He followed *The Charge of the Light Brigade* with *How I Won the War*. In the 1970s he wrote *Jingo* (1976), a play about the collapse of the British in Singapore in 1942. Further investigations of the army and the British Empire followed, and then in 1984 he wrote *Tumbledown* for the BBC. The play explored the way in which the Falklands campaign transformed the life of a cocky, young Scots Guards officer. Richard Eyre noted of it: 'his subject matter is so uncompromisingly painful and tells such uncomfortable truths about mankind – or at least about men'.[63] But, like *The Charge of the Light Brigade*, it also revealed the language, codes and customs of close-knit, closed societies. Wood's command of the idiom of army, empire and class has remained masterly.

RICHARDSON'S SUBSEQUENT CAREER

With *The Charge of the Light Brigade* hardly the financial success United Artists wanted and Woodfall dividing following the estrangement from Osborne, Richardson was caught in a potentially odd situation. Just what was he to do next? Fortunately, sheer enthusiasm for the thrill of directing rarely left him, but his next project was hardly one he expected. His agent Robin Fox put Nabokov's novella *Laughter in the Dark* in front of him. After the huge scale of *The Charge* it must have seemed a strangely compact and restraining idea. At first Richardson was reluctant, but changed his mind. Never one to do things conventionally, he planned to set the story in the contemporary art world. United Artists could not have been that disillusioned with him, for they agreed to finance the project. Richard Burton's warm response to Richardson's invitation to play the lead might well have fired the enthusiasm.

Burton arrived in London with Elizabeth Taylor and they set up home in the Dorchester. Taylor offered her services as an extra in an art auction scene. Thinking it would make for a jolly working atmosphere Richardson agreed, only to find that Taylor wanted £10,000 for her day's work. Knowing the budget could not support the demand he was forced to decline her offer. Mulling over the matter she agreed to appear for free if she could have an outfit made by a Paris couturier. Again Richardson had to refuse the offer. Eventually, Taylor turned up in a scene-stealing outfit of her own and duly did just that. It makes for a good anecdote, but it did not bode well for the film itself.

Things got worse. Burton turned on a prima donna routine, taking hours off for lunch, leaving early and sneering at the script. Richardson's patience snapped when Burton did not appear for a shoot until noon. Exploding with rage, he informed Burton he was in breach of contract and was fired. United Artists agreed to back Richardson's decision and Nicol Williamson was procured as a replacement. The film was finally back on track, but the final version does not hold together well. William-son is fine in the lead role, but this is an occasion when the novelty of setting and style do not gel, leaving a mess. United Artists did not give the film much publicity and it made very little money. It signalled the retreat of Hollywood companies from risky projects, particularly risky British projects.

Richardson returned to the theatre and capitalised on the relationship he had built up with Nicol Williamson for a production of *Hamlet*. It did excellent business in London and was then taken to the USA where it achieved a more modest success, but was a success none the less. With a fit of energy Richardson decided to see through this experiment in Shakespeare. Frustrated at the way cinematic versions of Shakespeare reduced the world of the imagination by realising every image, and yet not wanting to make a filmed stage play, he conceived of a bold experi-ment. He got backing for a film and shot it at the Roundhouse theatre *after* the actors had given their evening performance. For ten gruelling days the shooting continued, but a little gem had been polished up. Forcing the actors to concentrate on their lines and shooting them mainly in close-up, the film has a real intensity and once again Richardson defied simple classification – it is not a Shakespeare film in the sense of

Olivier's productions, but neither is it a filmed stage play. Costing about £200,000 it earned double that amount and the experience of making money for a change must have been good.

The next project could not have been more different. This time Richardson went back to the strange landscapes he found so fascinating. Ned Kelly, the famous Australian bandit who donned his own home-made armour, is certainly a great subject for a movie. It was a story Richardson had been toying with for some time. Both he and Karel Reisz had seen the Australian artist Sidney Nolan's paintings of the outlaw in the early 1960s. Richardson planned the movie as an extended visual ballad, but wanted to see the Australian bush first. He and Neil Hartley, a member of the Woodfall company and producer of *The Charge of the Light Brigade*, travelled out to Australia to explore. The trip appears to have been an absolute hoot as the people of the outback lived up to their stereotype of being fearsome drinkers. Mick Jagger was then cast in the lead. It was an unhappy experiment, for though Jagger's face looked right, the rest of him was all wrong. Richardson was forced to admit as much: 'Having gone for Mick, I should have made a very different kind of film – maybe a kind of collage that capitalized on the striking contrasts of his talent, instead of trying to push Mick into being an incipient John Wayne.'[64]

Around this time Richardson's domestic life fell into a state of flux. He and Vanessa Redgrave had parted and he was about to set up home in California. Despite these upheavals his appetite remained high and in 1977 he started work on another adaptation of Fielding, *Joseph Andrews*. David Watkin's photography of the English countryside was ravishing and an excellent cast was assembled including John Gielgud, Michael Hordern, Peggy Ashcroft and Beryl Reid. In the USA it was promoted with only mild enthusiasm and as some sort of sequel to *Tom Jones*. It made the film appear old-fashioned in every sense and so was not a great success.

Versatility was always Richardson's trademark and his next major project, *The Border* (1982), grew out of plans to make a version of Graham Greene's *A Gun for Sale*. Thanks to a series of twists and turns a new project based upon the US border patrol of the frontier with Mexico eventually resulted. Jack Nicholson and Harvey Keitel starred in this tough little movie. It feels more like an expanded documentary piece, with a strong sense of the dichotomy of having the world's richest nation existing alongside one of the poorest.

Three years later he made *The Hotel New Hampshire*, based on John

Irving's novel. It starred the young actors Rob Lowe, Jody Foster and Natasha Kinski. A seemingly modern piece, the film actually has under-tones of Dickens and Fielding in the sense of its use of large characters with fine details. Richardson gave this story about family life a feeling of fairy-tale, especially in his use of the 'Barcarole' from Offenbach's *Tales of Hoffmann*. Once again the critics were baffled – it was certainly a long way from *The Border*, and yet was a modern-dress piece that almost disguised a costume drama. American critics hated it, but it received a better reception in Britain. Fortunately, it had been an in-expensive movie and so the savaging it received at the hands of the critics was not as disastrous as it could have been.

Richardson continued to be active throughout the 1980s, making pieces for US television, including a version of *The Phantom of the Opera* (1990). He died in 1991 with his last film, *Blue Sky*, unreleased. A talented and hugely imaginative director, Richardson never quite achieved the same power and intensity after *The Charge of the Light Brigade*. In fact, there is a good deal more truth to the criticism that he became an erratic force *after* making *The Charge of the Light Brigade*. Perhaps the problem was that he lost his greatest collaborators and colleagues. Without John Osborne, Karel Reisz and Charles Wood to bounce off, shape and create with he was not the force he had been. Or rather he was the force he always had been, only now it lacked the critical input any great energy and talent needs to flourish properly.

Conclusion

The Charge of the Light Brigade is a deeply impressive piece of work. It is committed and energetic, it is beautiful to look at and powerful and moving. It is also a strange mix of different themes and threads. Without a doubt it is easy to pick holes in it. The lack of a sympathetic hero to identify with certainly flies in the face of filmic convention. The shocking, abrupt ending also leaves the viewer rather numbed. Kevin Brownlow wanted the film to end with the army marching off, trumpets blaring, colours and standards flying. He believed this would have served two purposes: it would provide an up-beat ending for a battered audience, while also retaining a highly ironic edge, reflecting the actual campaign.[1] After all, the charge did not end the war nor the blunders. The British army simply moved on and took the whole fiasco in its stride.

History provided a lesson and parable for the present in *The Charge of the Light Brigade*. Victorian Britain came to the 1960s in the brilliant performances of the cast and the wonderful camerawork, set and costume designs. Unfortunately for Woodfall and United Artists, the cinema-going public was not in the mood for such a strange sermon. A work of art had certainly been created. Kevin Brownlow appreciated the bold attempt to explore cinematically the idiom of mid-Victorian Britain. He wrote: 'In this era of computerised film-making when practically anything with pictures is accepted as camerawork, some dedicated film-makers had tried to achieve something completely new.'[2] Written in 1968, these notes reveal the feeling that film-making had become a 'paint by numbers' affair against which Tony Richardson and his team had fought valiantly.

Without a doubt the team assembled by Richardson appreciated the chance to make the film. Kevin Brownlow, David Watkin and Charles Wood stressed the tremendous dedication shown by all involved in the project. All three also stressed the enthusiasm and drive of Richardson himself. Few of the cast and crew had worked with such zeal and in such a great atmosphere. For Watkin, Wood and Brownlow – who have all achieved considerable success within the film, theatrical and television world on prestigious projects – *The Charge of the Light Brigade* remains a happy and proud memory. 'It was the most enjoyable thing I have ever done,' said Brownlow at one point when interviewed. Without prompting he twice returned to this theme: 'It was a joy to work on', and he recalled his 'gloriously happy memory' of it.[3] Equally obvious was Watkin's joyous recall of the project; he had nothing but happy memories of a team pulling hard to make a fine film.[4] Charles Wood wrote:

> I probably had the best working relationship with Tony that I've ever had with any director before or since, but that was true, I think, of all of us. He had a genius for the kind of leadership that gets a film made … I enjoyed being involved in making the film more than any film or play before or since. It was, in my opinion, 'total' film-making, everybody felt that they were doing something extraordinary.[5]

But panegyric should not blind us to the faults of the film. That is not the point of this exploration. Rather, it is to argue that the film is great, despite its faults. *The Charge of the Light Brigade* challenges its viewers to come to terms with it, while at the same time it beguiles, intrigues and charms them. Victorian Britain is brought to life in a wonderful tapestry, the atmosphere of 1960s Britain pervades the film in its almost gauche vitality and commitment. *The Charge of the Light Brigade* is not perfect by any means, but it is splendid. Lurid, splendid and, rather ironically, romantic in its audacity.

Notes

1. THE CONTEXT

1. All biographical references to Richardson's life are taken from Richardson, *Long Distance Runner*.
2. Ibid., p. 79.
3. Ibid., p. 69.
4. Quoted in Marwick, *Culture in Britain Since 1945*, p. 75.
5. Figures from Murphy, *Sixties British Cinema*, p. 21.
6. Ibid., p. 22.
7. Quoted in ibid., p. 24.
8. Ibid., p. 4.
9. Ibid., pp. 112–13.
10. Ibid., p. 5.
11. Ibid., p. 65.
12. Clark, *The Donkeys*, p. 11.
13. Kevin Brownlow, notebook, 18 April 1968. (Hereafter, 'Brownlow notes'.)
14. See Wiener, *English Culture and the Decline of the Industrial Spirit*.
15. Orwell, 'The Lion and the Unicorn', pp. 148–9.
16. Brooke-Taylor, *Rule Britannia*, p. 109.
17. Except where otherwise noted, the story of the making has been taken from Richardson, *Long Distance Runner*, pp. 193–201.
18. Ibid., pp. 9, 193.
19. See Murphy, *Sixties British Cinema*, pp. 256–75. Also see Walker, *Hollywood England*.
20. Richardson, *Long Distance Runner*, p. 194.
21. Charles Wood, email to author, 14 August 2000. (Hereafter, 'Wood, email'.)
22. Wood, 'Into the Valley', p. 26.
23. Wood, email.
24. Wood, 'Into the Valley', p. 26.
25. Richardson, *Long Distance Runner*, p. 194.
26. *The Sun*, 21 March 1967.
27. Wood, 'Into the Valley', p. 26.
28. Ibid.

29. Ibid.

30. Interview with Kevin Brownlow, 27 June 2000. (Hereafter, 'Brownlow, interview'.)

31. Interview with David Watkin, 27 July 2000. (Hereafter, 'Watkin, interview'.)

32. Wood, email.

33. Brownlow, interview.

34. Watkin, interview.

35. Ibid.

36. Wood, email.

37. *Daily Sketch*, 25 August 1965.

38. Richardson, *Long Distance Runner*, p. 195.

39. Watkin, interview.

40. Richardson, *Long Distance Runner*, p. 197; Watkin, interview; Radovitch, *Tony Richardson*, p. 25.

41. Gielgud, *An Actor and his Time*, p. 195.

42. Ibid.

43. Munn, *Trevor Howard*, p. 119.

44. Ibid., p. 120.

45. Watkin, interview.

46. Lellis, 'Recent Richardson', p. 133.

47. Watkin, interview.

48. Munn, *Trevor Howard*, p. 119.

49. Brownlow notes; Brownlow interview.

50. Richardson, *Long Distance Runner*, p. 200.

51. Brownlow, interview.

52. Watkin, interview.

53. *Daily Mail* 27 December 1967.

54. Richardson, *Long Distance Runner*, p. 201.

2. THE NARRATIVE

1. Medhurst, 'War Games', p. 28.

2. Woodham-Smith's history shows that Nolan actually joined Cardigan only at the very last moment. However Cardigan did have a long history of arguing with his officers, particularly if he felt they had more experience than he did. Much of the plot concerning his arguments with Nolan actually refers to his running feud with Captain Wathen. See Woodham-Smith, *The Reason Why*, pp. 43–4.

3. In the film this exchange takes place between Cardigan and Squire de Burgh, excellently played by Willoughby Goddard. The Squire also accompanies Cardigan to the Crimea. Woodham-Smith gives details of the friendship be-

tween the two men, showing that Wood perfectly captured the nature of their relationship. See Woodham-Smith, *The Reason Why*, pp. 133, 205–7.

4. See ibid., p. 172 for details of Nolan's horse training system and his commitment to 'gentleness'.

5. Wood, 'Into the Valley', p. 26.

6. Wood, email.

7. The black bottle incident was actually the result of Cardigan's long-running feud with Captain John Reynolds, an Indian Army officer who had joined his regiment. Woodham-Smith gives full details of the row and incidents in which 'black bottle' was chanted at Cardigan. See Woodham-Smith, *The Reason Why*, pp. 61–7.

8. Watkin, interview.

9. Cardigan had employed his men as spies during the feud with Captain Wathen. See Woodham-Smith, *The Reason Why*, p. 43.

10. Cardigan created a scandal by ordering the flogging of a trooper immediately after Church Parade on Easter Sunday 1841. See Woodham-Smith, *The Reason Why*, p. 89.

11. For details of Raglan's obsession with the duke, see Woodham-Smith, *The Reason Why*, pp. 159, 161.

12. Watkin interview. See also David Watkin, *Why is There Only One Word for Thesaurus?*, pp. 125–35.

13. See Woodham-Smith, *The Reason Why*, pp. 232–4.

14. Ibid., p. 240.

15. Ibid., p. 249 and p 253.

16. Ibid., p. 254.

17. See Jeffrey Richards, *Visions of Yesterday*, pp. 57, 125–6, for more details about Flynn's role in imperial movies and the nature of the plot.

3. THE RECEPTION AND THE YEARS THAT FOLLOWED

1. *The Times*, 9 April 1968.

2. *The Sun*, 9 April 1968.

3. *New Statesman*, 12 April 1968.

4. *Guardian*, 10 April 1968.

5. *Evening News*, 10 April 1968.

6. *Evening Standard*, 11 April 1968; *Daily Express*, 13 April 1968; *Sunday Telegraph*, 14 April 1968; *The Sun*, 13 April 1968.

7. *Guardian*, 13 April 1968.

8. *Daily Express*, 13 April 1968.

9. *Sunday Telegraph*, 14 April 1968.

10. *Evening Standard*, 11 April 1968.

11. Brownlow, notes.

12. Quotations taken from *Key Profiles in Animation: Richard Williams*, no imprint, 1972, a folder of loose sheets in the British Film Institute Library.

13. *Sunday People*, 14 April 1968.

14. *Kine Weekly*, 17 April 1968.

15. *Monthly Film Bulletin*, July 1968, p. 98.

16. Wood, email.

17. *New York Times*, 7 October 1968.

18. *Variety*, 17 April 1968.

19. *Kine Weekly*, 20 April 1968.

20. *Kine Weekly*, 18 May 1968.

21. *Kine Weekly*, 22 June 1968.

22. *Kine Weekly*, 29 June 1968; 6 July 1968; 20 July 1968; 27 July 1968; 3 August 1968; 10 August 1968; 17 August 1968; 24 August 1968.

23. *Kine Weekly*, 3 August 1968.

24. Craddock, '*The Charge of the Light Brigade* in Perspective', p. 14.

25. Brownlow, interview.

26. Richardson, *Long Distance Runner*, p. 200.

27. Walker, *Hollywood England*, p. 367.

28. Lellis, 'Recent Richardson'.

29. Brownlow, interview.

30. Wood, email.

31. Watkin, interview.

32. Nowlan and Nowlan, *Cinema Sequels and Remakes*, p. 138.

33. Craddock, '*The Charge of the Light Brigade* in Perspective', p. 15.

34. Brownlow, interview.

35. Fraser, *The Hollywood History of the World*, p. 161.

36. Walker, *Hollywood England*, p. 367.

37. Lellis, 'Recent Richardson', p. 130.

38. Wood, 'Into the Valley', p. 28.

39. Craddock, '*The Charge of the Light Brigade* in Perspective', p. 14.

40. Fraser, *The Hollywood History of the World*, p. 161.

41. Eyre (ed.), *Charles Wood Plays, One*, p. 8.

42. Medhurst, 'War Games', p. 29.

43. Richards, conversation with the author, 3 December 1999.

44. Lellis, 'Recent Richardson', p. 130.

45. Ibid., p. 131.

46. Craddock, '*The Charge of the Light Brigade* in Perspective', pp. 32–3.

47. Ibid., p. 15.

48. Redgrave, *An Autobiography*, p. 137; letter to author, 30 November 1999.

49. Munn, *Trevor Howard*, p. 119.

50. Medhurst, 'War Games', p. 30.

51. Richards, *Visions of Yesterday*, p. 126.

52. Craddock, '*The Charge of the Light Brigade* in Perspective', p. 15.

53. Wood, email.

54. Craddock, '*The Charge of the Light Brigade* in Perspective', p. 33.

55. Ibid., p. 34.

56. Lellis, 'Recent Richardson', p. 130.

57. Craddock, '*The Charge of the Light Brigade* in Perspective', p. 15.

58. Wood, *Veterans*, in Eyre (ed.), *Charles Wood Plays, One*, p. 53.

59. Munn, *Trevor Howard*, pp. 117–20.

60. Wood, *Veterans*, in Eyre (ed.), *Charles Wood Plays, One*, p. 62.

61. Ibid., p. 19.

62. Ibid., pp. 22–3.

63. Eyre in ibid., p. 9.

64. Richardson, *Long Distance Runner*, p. 224.

CONCLUSION

1. Brownlow, interview.

2. Brownlow, notes.

3. Brownlow, interview.

4. Watkin, interview.

5. Wood, email. Interestingly, Wood also wanted to give praise and thanks to Osborne. He added: 'I am very grateful to John Osborne for handing it to me and I never stopped telling him so. But it was his film as well. He always felt that and so did I.'

Tony Richardson, a Filmography

Momma Don't Allow (UK 1955)

Look Back in Anger (UK 1959)

The Entertainer (UK 1960)

Saturday Night and Sunday Morning (UK 1960, Producer)

Sanctuary (USA 1961)

A Taste of Honey (UK 1961)

The Loneliness of the Long Distance Runner (UK 1962)

Tom Jones (UK 1963)

Girl with Green Eyes (UK 1964, Executive Producer)

The Loved One (USA 1965)

Mademoiselle (UK/France 1966)

The Sailor from Gibraltar (UK 1967)

Red and Blue (UK 1967)

The Charge of the Light Brigade (UK 1968)

Hamlet (UK 1969)

Laughter in the Dark (UK/France 1969)

Ned Kelly (UK 1970)

A Delicate Balance (USA 1973)

Dead Cert (UK 1974)

Joseph Andrews (UK 1977)

A Death in Canaan (USA 1978)

The Border (USA 1982)

The Hotel New Hampshire (USA 1984)

Penalty Phase (USA 1986)

Shadow in the Sun (USA 1988)

Hills Like White Elephants (USA 1990)

Blue Sky (USA 1990)

Bibliography

Brooke-Taylor, Tim, *Rule Britannia: The Ways and World of the True British Gentleman Patriot* (London, 1983).

Clark, Alan, *The Donkeys* (London, 1961).

Craddock, John, '*The Charge of the Light Brigade* in Perspective', *Film Society Review*, 4 (7), March 1969.

Eyre, Richard (ed.), *Charles Wood Plays, One: Veterans; Across from the Garden of Allah* (London, 1997).

Fraser, George MacDonald, *The Hollywood History of the World* (London, 1988).

Gielgud, John, *An Actor and his Time* (London, 1979).

Hichberger, J. M. W., *Images of the Army: The Military in British Art, 1815–1914* (Manchester, 1988).

Judd, Denis, *The Crimean War* (London, 1976).

Lalumia, Matthew Paul, *Realism and Politics in Victorian Art of the Crimean War* (Ann Arbor, MI, 1984).

Lellis, George, 'Recent Richardson: Cashing the Blank Cheque', *Sight and Sound*, 38, Summer 1969.

Marwick, Arthur, *Culture in Britain Since 1945* (Oxford, 1991).

Medhurst, Andy, 'War Games', *Sight and Sound*, 2 (1), May 1992.

Munn, Michael, *Trevor Howard: The Man and his Films* (London, 1989).

Murphy, Robert, *Sixties British Cinema* (London, 1992).

Nowlan, Robert and Gwendolyn Wright Nowlan, *Cinema Sequels and Remakes, 1903–1987* (Jefferson, NC, 1989).

Orwell, George, 'The Lion and the Unicorn', in *The Essays of George Orwell* (Harmondsworth, 1984).

Radovitch, Don, *Tony Richardson: A Bio-bibliography* (London, 1995).

Redgrave, Vanessa, *An Autobiography* (London, 1992).

— 'Tony Richardson and *The Charge of the Light Brigade*', *Sight and Sound*, 2 (1), May 1992.

Richards, Jeffrey, *Visions of Yesterday* (London, 1974).

Richardson, Tony, *Long Distance Runner: A Memoir* (London, 1992).

Walker, Alexander: *Hollywood England: The British Film Industry in the Sixties* (London, 1974).

Watkin, David, *Why is There Only One Word for Thesaurus?* (Brighton, 1998).

Wiener, Martin, *English Culture and the Decline of the Industrial Spirit* (Cambridge, 1981).

Wood, Charles, 'Into the Valley', *Sight and Sound*, 2 (1), May 1992.

Woodham-Smith, Cecil, *The Reason Why* (London, 1953).

JOURNALS AND NEWSPAPERS

Daily Cinema; *Daily Express*; *Daily Mirror*; *Daily Sketch*; *Evening Standard*; *Guardian*; *Illustrated London News*; *Kine Weekly*; *New Statesman*; *New York Times*; *People*; *Sun*; *Sunday Telegraph*; *Sunday Times*; *The Times*; *Variety*.

INTERVIEWS AND CORRESPONDENCE

Kevin Brownlow, 27 June 2000.

Vanessa Redgrave, 30 November 1999.

David Watkin, 27 July 2000.

Charles Wood, 14 August 2000.

UNPUBLISHED MATERIAL

Kevin Brownlow, notebooks.

Key Profiles in Animation: Richard Williams in the British Film Institute Library.